# THE PRAYING MOTHER:

## GATEKEEPER'S WOMB

**The "Touch Not" Mandate for Family Deliverance and Breaking Generational Strongholds**

**Dr. Philomena Gerald**

## Dedication

To the **Mothers who refuse to sleep** while the enemy is at the gate; to the women who have turned their bedrooms into war rooms and their tears into liquid fire.

To my children, my **Lions and Lionesses**, who were carried in prayer before they were carried in my arms. You are the reason the wall was built. You are the "Touch Not" generation, the Governors of tomorrow, and the joy of my today.

To the **Father of Lights**, who entrusted the womb to the woman and gave us the Gavel to protect the Seed.

And finally, to **You, the Reader**: May this book find you at your post. Whether you are in the season of pregnancy, the labor of raising toddlers, or the standing watch over adult children, may you realize that you are not just a parent; you are a **Gatekeeper**.

As you turn these pages, may your "Tent Peg" be sharpened, your discernment be deepened, and your family throne be permanently established.

**For the Seed. For the Throne. For the Kingdom.**

*"Her children arise and call her blessed; her husband also, and he praises her: 'Many women do noble things, but you surpass them all.'"* **Proverbs 31:28-29**

## Preface

The world has long celebrated the tenderness of a mother, but it has largely forgotten her **terribleness** in the face of the enemy.

For too long, the "praying mother" has been depicted as a passive figure of quiet sighs and gentle hopes. But the spiritual reality is far more severe. A mother is the first line of defense; she is the **Gatekeeper of the Womb** and the **Chief Security Officer of the Home**. She is the only human being on earth given the legal, biological, and spiritual right to carry a destiny within her own body for nine months, a season of "Divine Incubation" that grants her a lifelong mandate to legislate for that soul.

This book is born out of a burden for the **Seed**.

We live in an age where the "House of Ahab" and the "Systems of Jezebel" are actively hunting the virtues of our children before they can even speak. From the moment of conception, a "Marine Warfare" is launched against their stars, their health, and their identities. The enemy knows that if he can corrupt the foundation, he doesn't have to fight the building. If he can exchange the virtue in the womb, he can occupy the throne in the future.

**But he did not account for You.**

In these pages, we move beyond "survival prayers." We are shifting from asking God to "protect" our children to decreeing that they are **Untouchable**. We are transitioning from being mothers who worry to being **Governors who Rule**.

You will learn that your prayer is the spiritual "umbilical cord" that continues to feed your children long after the physical one is cut. You will discover how to use the "Tent Peg" of Jael to strike the head of territorial oppressors and how to sanitize your bloodline from ancestral traps that have plagued your lineage for generations.

I am writing this to the mother who is tired of seeing her children struggle with the same "Normalised Evil" that attacked her parents. I am writing this to the woman who is currently pregnant and feels the weight of the "Lion" she is carrying. I am writing to the "Deborahs" who are ready to arise and shout, **"Not on my watch!"**

As you read, you will find that you are not just raising "kids." You are raising **Governors, Lions, and Lionesses.** You are preserving **Thrones.** You are establishing a **"Touch Not" Generation** that will walk through the fire of this world and not even smell like smoke.

The Gate is closed. The Blood is applied. The Fire is lit.

**Mother, it is time to occupy your post.**
**Dr. Philomena Gerald**

# Table of Contents


Introduction .......... 9

[illegible]

# Table of Contents

Introduction.......................................................................... 9

The Midnight Cry at the Gate................................................. 9

Chapter 1: The Spiritual Umbilical Cord ............................ 13

Why 9 Months of Carrying Grants You 90 Years of Legislating................................................................................. 13

Chapter 2: The Mother at The Gate...................................... 22

*The Legal Authority to Open and Shut Doors for Your Household*................................................................................. 22

Chapter 3: Guarding The Incubation.................................... 30

*Shielding the Womb from Miscarriages, Disorders, and the Theft of Virtues*.................................................................... 30

Chapter 4: The Labor of Prayer............................................. 38

*Birthing the Destiny of Your Children through Spiritual Travail*....................................................................................... 38

Chapter 5: Raising Lions and Lionesses............................... 46

*Shifting from "Survival Prayers" to "Throne Room Decrees"* ............................................................................................. 46

Chapter 6: Uprooting The Unwanted Seed.......................... 51

*Extracting "Normalized Evil" Before It Takes Root in Their Character*.................................................................................. 51

Chapter 7: Guarding The Marriage Bed .............................. 56

*Protecting the Atmosphere of the Home from Intruding Spirits*....................................................................................... 56

Chapter 8: Bloodline Sanitation ........................................... 63

*Scrubbing Corrupted Foundations from Both Maternal and Paternal Lineages* ........63

Chapter 9: The Spiritual Map ........68

*Gaining Discernment to See the Traps in your destiny, throne, star, Academics, Health, and Social Circles* ........68

Chapter 10: Breaking Lineage Traps ........78

*Disconnecting Your Sons and Daughters from Ancestral Cycles* ........78

Chapter 11: The "Touch Not" Generation........88

*Encasing Your Family in the Wall of Fire and the Blood of the Lamb*........88

Chapter 12: Virtue Recovery ........98

*Reclaiming Every Star, Gift, and Inheritance the Enemy Attempted to Exchange*........98

Chapter 13: Securing The Virtues........106

*Locking in Wealth, Creativity, and Longevity Before Adulthood*........106

Chapter 14: The Power of Consistency........116

*Preventing Addictions and Soul Ties Through Disciplined Prayer*........116

Chapter 15: From The Nursery to The Nation........124

*How a Stable, Praying Home Heals the World* ........124

The Governor's War Room: Prayer ........135

DECLARATIONS:........138

# Introduction

## The Midnight Cry at the Gate

There is a sound currently echoing through the corridors of the spirit, it is not a sound of defeat, but the roar of a mother who has realized who she is. For twenty years, Sisera oppressed Israel, and the highways were abandoned. Travelers took to the winding paths because the main roads were too dangerous. This is the state of many families today. Our children are taking "winding paths" of addiction, confusion, and identity crisis because the spiritual highways of our lineages have been occupied by territorial oppressors.

But Judges 5:7 tells us when the atmosphere shifted: ***"Village life ceased, it ceased in Israel, until I, Deborah, arose, arose a mother in Israel."***

Notice it doesn't say she arose as a General or a Judge, though she was both. She arose as a **Mother**. There is a specific frequency of authority that is only unlocked when a woman moves from the "worry of the heart" to the "warfare of the spirit."

### The Architecture of the Womb

The womb is not merely an organ; it is the first **Courtroom of Destiny**. It is where the "Technical Manual" of a child's life is first written by the finger of God. However, because the enemy is a thief of virtues, he attempts to infiltrate this sacred incubation period. He knows that if he can plant a seed of disorder, a spirit of infirmity, or a "Marine Exchange" while the child is still being knit together in secret, he can claim ownership before the child even takes their first breath.

Most mothers have been taught to pray for their children *after* the problem manifests. We pray when the grades drop, when the marriage struggles, or when the addiction takes hold. But the **Gatekeeper's Womb** strategy is about **Preemptive Legislation**.

**Raising the Untouchable**

In this book, we are establishing a "Touch Not" mandate. This is not a suggestion; it is a judicial decree. To be "Touch Not" means your children are surrounded by a **Wall of Fire** that makes them spiritually radioactive to the kingdom of darkness. It means that when the enemy attempts to plant seeds of "Normalized Evil" in your son or daughter, he finds no soil to hold them.

As a **Governor** in the spirit, you have been given the Gavel to strike down every illegal lien placed on your children's virtues. Whether you are currently carrying a child, raising toddlers, or standing in the gap for adult children who have lost their way, the principles in these chapters will show you how to:

**Discern the Spiritual Map:** See the traps before your children walk into them.

**Sanitize the Bloodline:** Scrub the "Ahab" and "Jezebel" influences from their DNA.

**Secure the Throne:** Ensure your children don't just "survive" the world, but rule it as Lions and Lionesses.

**The Call to Arise**

Mother, you have gone through the pregnancy season and the labor season. You have felt the physical cost of bringing life into this world. Now, it is time to realize the spiritual weight of that sacrifice. You are the **Watchman**. You are the **Wall**. You are the reason the enemy will fail.

The days of our children being "wasted" are over. The days of "miscarriages of destiny" are finished. We are raising a generation that is soaked in the Blood and encased in Fire.

**Welcome to the Command Center. Let the Gatekeeper arise.**

**How to Use the Book?**

To get the maximum "Judicial Weight" and spiritual results from **"A Praying Mother, The Gatekeeper's Womb,"** you must treat it as more than a book. It is a **Manual of Operations** for your home.

Here is how to use this book to secure your family and raise your Lions and Lionesses:

**Use it as a "War Room" Blueprint**

Don't just read this book in bed; take it into your place of prayer.

**The Declarations:** At the end of every chapter, there are specific **Decrees.** Speak them out loud over your children's photos, their bedrooms, and even your own womb.

**The Gavel Strike:** When you reach the sections on **Lineage Deliverance**, use the written prayers as a legal petition. Stand in your authority as a Governor and "strike the gavel" against ancestral traps.

**Apply the "Rule of First Mention" (Pre-emptive Prayer)**

Use the chapters on **Guarding the Incubation** and **The Spiritual Map** to pray ahead of time.

If your children are babies, pray the "Throne and Crown" chapters now.

If you are pregnant, prioritize the "Virtue Guard" prayers to stop any spiritual exchange before birth.

**The Goal:** Stop the "Sisera" of their future before he ever mounts his chariot.

**The "Soaking" Method**

Since you are **"Soaking at the Feet of Jesus,"** use the wisdom in this book during your quiet time.

Read one chapter, then sit in silence (soaking).

Ask the Holy Spirit to show you the "Spiritual Map" of your child's life mentioned in **Chapter 7**.

Write down the names, specific virtues, or "Unwanted Seeds" the Spirit highlights to you.

**Consistent "Wall Building"**

As noted in **Chapter 9**, the power is in **Consistency**.
Do not wait for a crisis to open this book.
Use it to build a "Wall of Fire" daily.
Make it a habit to "Blood Soak" your children's academics, health, and future marriages every week using the templates provided.

**Identify the "Lion Identity"**

Use the book to change how you *speak* to your children.
After reading **Chapter 5**, stop calling them "kids" and start addressing them as **Governors, Lions, and Lionesses.** Teach them the "Touch Not" mandate. Let them hear you decreeing that they are "radioactive" to the enemy. This builds their own spiritual confidence.

**The Practical Schedule:**

**Phase 1 The Cleanse:** Focus on Chapters 6 and 10 (Bloodline and Lineage Traps) first to clear the foundation.
**Phase 2 The Shield:** Focus on Chapters 3, 5, and 11 to set up the "Wall of Fire."
**Phase 3 The Crown:** Focus on Chapters 8, 13, and 14 to secure their long term wealth, stars, and destiny.

**Governor's Note:** This book is your "Tent Peg." Use it to pin the enemy to the ground and establish your family in **Rehoboth**, the place where there is finally "room" for your children to flourish without strife.

**Are you ready to strike the first gavel?**

# Chapter 1: The Spiritual Umbilical Cord

## Why 9 Months of Carrying Grants You 90 Years of Legislating

In the natural world, the umbilical cord is a biological lifeline, a conduit through which a mother transfers oxygen, nutrients, and life sustaining blood to her developing child. However, in the realm of the spirit, this connection does not dissolve when the physical cord is severed in the delivery room.

Instead, it transitions into a **Spiritual Umbilical Cord**: a permanent, mystical, legal tether that grants a mother the high ranking authority to legislate over her child's destiny for the rest of their life.

### The Law of First Possession

### Jeremiah 1:5 The Pre Birth Jurisdiction

"Before I formed you in the womb I knew you; before you were born I sanctified you; I ordained you a prophet to the nations."

The spiritual world operates on legalities. The reason the enemy fights so hard for the womb is that he understands the **Law of First Possession**. Because you were the first human environment to house that soul, you hold the primary "title deed" to that child's foundational atmosphere.

**The 9-Month Incubation:** This is not just biological growth; it is a period of "Divine Squatting." You have occupied the space first.

**The Legal Precedent:** In spiritual jurisprudence, the person who provides the foundation has the greatest right to dictate the structure. Because your body provided the temple for that spirit to enter the earth, the Courts of Heaven recognize your voice as the primary legislative authority over that temple.

To deepen the revelation of **The Legal Precedent**, we must look at the mother's role as the **"Contractual Landlord"** of human entry. In the Courts of Heaven, authority is often tied to "Territorial Jurisdiction."

When you carried your child, you weren't just a biological host; you were the **Sovereign Territory** where that spirit was naturalized into the physical world.

**The Doctrine of "Entry Rights"**

In spiritual law, the way a spirit enters a realm determines who has legal oversight over it. Because the child entered the Earth-realm through *your* portal (your womb), you are the **Sponsor of Record**.

**The Divine Notary:** God used your body as the legal "Notary" to stamp that child's arrival. Because your blood, your breath, and your DNA formed the physical casing of that spirit, you hold a permanent "Lien" on their foundational structure.

**The Voice of the Foundation:** If a building begins to lean, the law doesn't look at the roof; it looks at the foundation. Because you *are* the foundation, the Courts of Heaven prioritize your testimony. When a mother speaks, she is speaking from the **Root Level**, which can override "surface level" attacks the enemy tries to implement later in life.

**First Occupancy and the "Right of Way"**

There is a concept in law called *Adverse Possession*, but in the spirit, we call it **Divine Occupancy**. By occupying the child's environment for 270 days (9 months), you established a "Right of Way."

**Evicting Squatters:** Because you occupied the space first, any demonic spirit that tries to influence your child later is legally a "squatter." A squatter has no title deed. You, as the mother, hold the **Title Deed of First Occupancy**.

**The Legislative Veto:** When the enemy brings a charge against your child, you can enter the Courtroom of Heaven and "Veto" the enemy's claim by citing the Law of First Possession. You can say: *"I was the first gate. I did not authorize this spirit of infirmity or Autism, or* *addiction or confusion to enter this temple during its formation. Therefore, its presence is a trespass."*

**The "Constitutional" Authority of the Womb**

Think of the 9 months in the womb as the drafting of the child's **Personal Constitution**.

Everything you prayed, whispered, and decreed during those 9 months became the "Original Intent" of that child's life.

In any court, the "Original Intent" of the founders carries the most weight. You are the **Founder of their physical existence**. When you legislate (pray) for them at age 20, 40, or 60, you are simply enforcing the "Original Constitutional Clauses" you established while they were in your womb.

**Silence as Consent (The Risk of the Gate)**

Because you are the primary legislative authority, spiritual law assumes that **what you do not forbid, you have permitted.** If a mother is silent, the enemy argues that the "Landlord" has abandoned the property, allowing him to move in.

**The Legislative Awakening:** This is why this book is vital. You are learning that your silence is a legal "Open Door," but your voice is a **Judicial Gavel**. When you speak, you are not just "wishing" for a blessing; you are **enforcing a title deed** that was signed the moment that child was conceived in your womb.

**The Governor's Judicial Brief**

"I decree that as the Founder and First Occupant of my child's foundational atmosphere, I hold the exclusive right to dictate the spiritual laws of their life. I invoke the 'Right of First Entry' and declare that any demonic lien, ancestral claim, or satanic contract seeking to attach itself to my child is Null and Void. I am the Sponsor of this destiny, and I only authorize the Kingdom of Light to legislate within this temple. The foundation is Holy, and the structure must follow! In Jesus' Name!" **Jeremiah 1:5**

### The Umbilical Conduit: Transferring More than DNA

While the child is in the womb, there is a total synchronization of systems. Your heart rhythm sets theirs; your peace becomes their chemical stability. Spiritually, this umbilical cord acts as a **Frequency Bridge**.

**Virtue Transfer:** During these nine months, you aren't just passing on physical traits like eye color; you are the gatekeeper for their **Virtues** and **Stars**.

**The Guarded Gate:** This chapter reveals that a mother can "filter" what passes through this spiritual cord. If a mother is unaware, ancestral baggage or "Marine Exchanges" can travel down this cord. But a **Praying Mother** uses the cord as a vacuum, pulling in divine grace and blocking out generational curses before the child is even born.

### The Frequency Bridge: Synchronizing Destinies

The mother's heart is the "Metronome" of the womb. In the spirit, this synchronization creates a **Frequency Bridge**.

**Emotional Imprinting:** If a mother dwells in fear, she is "broadcasting" that frequency directly into the child's spirit through the cord. However, the Praying Mother understands that she can intentionally set the frequency to **Kingdom Peace**.

**The Atmosphere of the Throne:** By maintaining a lifestyle of intercession, the mother ensures that the child's first experience of "reality" is the frequency of the Holy Spirit. You are literally tuning their spirit to recognize the voice of God before they ever hear a human voice.

### Virtue Transfer: Protecting the "Stars"

Every child is born with "Stars", divine virtues, talents, and the wealth of their destiny. In the Courts of Heaven, these are seen as **Spiritual Assets**.

**The Gatekeeper of Assets:** During these nine months, you are the temporary Trustee of these assets. The enemy often attempts a "Marine Exchange", a spiritual identity theft where a child's "Star" (their greatness) is swapped for a "Cloud" (obscurity or failure) while they are still in the womb.

**Locking the Virtues:** As the Gatekeeper, your prayers act as a **Security Encryption**. You aren't just passing on DNA; you are passing on a "Spiritual Blood Type" that is incompatible with failure. You are decreeing: *"That which God has put in this child, no man, no spirit, and no altar can take."*

### The Guarded Gate: The "Filtration System" of Prayer

The spiritual umbilical cord is bi directional. It can either be a highway for ancestral baggage or a vacuum for divine grace.

**Blocking the Ancestral Flow:** Without a praying mother, the cord can act as a "Sewer Pipe" through which generational curses, infirmities, patterns of divorce, or poverty, flow freely from the lineage into the new seed. This is how "Normalized Evil" is birthed into a new generation.

**The Vacuum of Grace:** The Praying Mother turns the cord into a **High Pressure Filter**. By the power of the Holy Spirit, she "vacuums" the treasures of the Kingdom into the child wisdom, favor, and health, while simultaneously creating a "Blockade" against the bloodline.

**The "Marine Exchange" Defense:** In deep deliverance, we know that "Marine Spirits" seek to claim the womb as their territory. But when a mother stands at the gate, she creates a **Spiritual Firewall**. She uses the umbilical cord to soak the child in the Blood of Jesus continually, making the child "spiritually slippery", the enemy cannot get a grip on their destiny.

### The Legislation of the Conduit

You have the legal right to dictate what "Data" is allowed to travel through the cord.

**The Protocol of Rejection:** You must consciously reject the "paternal baggage" and "maternal flaws" during the 9 months.
**The Protocol of Infusion:** You must intentionally speak the Word into the cord. You are "uploading" the scriptures into the child's subconscious. This is why children of praying mothers often have an "unexplained" inclination toward the things of God, they were "programmed" through the spiritual conduit before they were born.

### The Watchman's Decree

"I strike the Gavel over the conduit of life! I decree that this umbilical cord is a Sanctified Highway. I activate the Blood Filter now! I forbid any ancestral baggage, any marine exchange, and any foundational corruption from traveling into my seed. I vacuum the virtues of the Kingdom into this child's DNA. I lock their 'Star' into the heavens and decree it shall never be dimmed or traded. Every drop of blood flowing between us is purified by the Fire of the Holy Ghost! What was 'normal' in my lineage ends with me; what is 'divine' begins with them! In Jesus' Name!" **Hebrews 12:24** "To Jesus the Mediator of the new covenant, and to the sprinkled blood that speaks a better word than the blood of Abel."

### The 9:90 Ratio: The Longevity of the Mandate

Many mothers believe their influence wanes once the child becomes an adult. This is a deception. The **9:90 Principle** states that the intensity of the 9 month incubation creates a "Legal Momentum" that lasts for 90 years (the average lifetime).
**Legislating from the Root:** Because you were there at the *root* (conception), you have the authority to speak to the *fruit* (adulthood).
**Distance is Irrelevant:** Just as the spirit world knows no space, the spiritual umbilical cord knows no distance. Whether your child is in the next room or across the globe, your decree travels through this

established tether. When you speak, the spirit of that child "remembers" the authority of the one who first gave them life.

### Legislating from the Root: The Power of Origin

In any judicial system, the "Court of Original Jurisdiction" holds the primary record. Because you were the presiding authority at the **Root** (the womb), your voice carries a weight that can bypass the "Fruit" (the adult personality).

**The Root to Fruit Command:** When a child reaches adulthood, they develop their own will, and the enemy often uses this to build "surface level" strongholds like rebellion or poor choices. However, these are merely the "fruit." As the mother, you have the legal right to ignore the outward behavior and speak directly to the **root** of their existence which you helped form.

**Overriding the Timeline:** You are not just praying for who they are today; you are enforcing the "Original Intent" of who they were designed to be in the womb. Because you were there at the beginning, you have the authority to pull them back to their original divine blueprint, no matter how far they have strayed.

### Distance is Irrelevant: The Quantum Tether

The spiritual umbilical cord is not a physical rope; it is a **Quantum Tether** of the spirit. In the realm of God, there is no "here" or "there."

**The Frequency of Authority:** Your child's spirit was "imprinted" with your spiritual frequency during the nine month synchronization. When you decree a word in your prayer closet, that tether vibrates at the speed of thought.

**The Spirit's Memory:** Even if your child is thousands of miles away or emotionally distant, their **spirit** is legally bound to "remember" the authority of the life giver. When you speak, you are not shouting into the air; you are sending a judicial summons through a private, established conduit that the enemy cannot jam.

## Legal Momentum: The Law of Perpetual Motion

In physics, an object in motion stays in motion unless acted upon by an outside force. Your nine months of carrying created a **Legal Momentum.**

**The 90-Year Mandate:** The investment you made during those 270 days (9 months) didn't just stop at birth. It set a "trajectory" for the next 90 years.

**The Outside Force:** The enemy tries to be the "outside force" that stops your child's momentum. But as the Watchman, your decree acts as a **Propellant**, ensuring that the momentum of the womb carries them into their old age. You are legislating for their mid-life, their career, and their grandchildren's heritage before they even finish school.

Proverbs 22:6"Train up a child in the way he should go, and when he is old he will not depart from it."

**The Judicial Link:** This is the "Statute of Longevity" for the 9:90 Principle. The word "train" also means to "dedicate" or "inaugurate" it specifically refers to the narrowing of the palate or the "initiating" of a foundation.

**The "When He Is Old" Clause:** This scripture proves that the "initialization" (the 9 months) has a direct legal effect on the "old age" (the 90 years). It guarantees that the mandate you established at the **Root** creates a permanent "Way" that the spirit of the child is legally obligated to follow. It is a promise that your legislative authority outlasts their childhood and governs their entire lifespan.

## The Watchman's Decree of Longevity

"I strike the Gavel and invoke the 9:90 Principle over my seed! I decree that the mandate I established at the Root of their life shall govern the Fruit of their adulthood. I command every word I spoke in the secret place of the womb to manifest in their 20s, their 50s, and their 80s. I declare that distance is an illusion my voice travels through the spiritual tether and arrests their spirit for God's purpose, regardless of where they are on this earth. I enforce Proverbs 22:6: they shall not, they cannot, and they will not depart from the Way! The momentum of my prayer outlasts the season of their growth. In Jesus' Name!"

### The Power of the "Blood Tether"

The umbilical cord is, at its core, a blood connection. In the Kingdom, the **Life is in the Blood**.

By applying the Blood of Jesus to your spiritual umbilical cord, you create a "Sanitized Corridor." This means that even if the father's side of the lineage carries "corrupted data" (patterns, negative cycles, addiction, failure, or premature death), the mother can use her legislative right to act as a **Blood Filter**, ensuring that only the "New Covenant DNA" reaches the child.

### The Watchman's Decree

"I strike the Gavel and declare that my spiritual umbilical cord is a consecrated highway of light! I invoke my 9-month legal right to legislate over the next 90 years of my child's life. I decree that no familiar spirit can travel this cord, and no ancestral baggage can be transferred. I am the Gatekeeper of this bloodline, and I command every virtue intended for my seed to be delivered intact, without exchange or delay! In the name of Jesus, the mandate is set!" **Isaiah 49:25** "But thus says the Lord: 'Even the captives of the mighty shall be taken away, and the prey of the terrible be delivered; for I will contend with him who contends with you, and I will save your children.'"

## Chapter 2: The Mother at The Gate

### *The Legal Authority to Open and Shut Doors for Your Household*

In the ancient world, the "Gate" of a city was not just a point of entry; it was the **Seat of Government**. It was the place where elders sat, where contracts were signed, where judgments were rendered, and where the security of the entire city was determined.

In the spirit, the home is a city state, and the **Mother is the Gatekeeper**. You are the one stationed at the threshold between the spiritual realm and your family's physical reality. This chapter reveals that your position is not passive; it is a **Judicial Office**.

**The Power of "Legal Entry" and "Illegal Trespass"**

Everything that enters your home whether it is a spirit of peace, a spirit of infirmity, or a spirit of lack must pass through a "Gate."

**The Mother's Voice as a Key:** In spiritual jurisprudence, your permission is often required for a spirit to gain a foothold in your children's lives. If you do not consciously **Shut the Gate** against an ancestral pattern, the spirit world interprets your silence as "Legal Consent."

**The Watchman's Duty:** To "Shut the Door" means to issue a spiritual injunction that makes it impossible for an entity to function within your walls. You have the right to declare a "No-Fly Zone" over your children's minds and your husband's health.

To explore **"The Mother at the Gate"** through the lens of spiritual jurisprudence, we must understand that the home is a **Sovereign Estate**. In the spirit realm, rights of entry are governed by laws of "Consent" and "Covenant."

As the Mother at the Gate, you are the **Chief Security Officer** and the **Clerk of the Court** for your household. You are the one who determines which "Spiritual Visas" are approved and which are denied.

### The Power of "Legal Entry" and "Illegal Trespass"

In the natural world, a locksmith can tell you that a door only opens with the right key. In the spirit, the "Key" is **Authorization.**

**The Legal Entry:** A spirit of peace enters because it finds an environment that "matches" its frequency an environment authorized by prayer and worship.

**The Illegal Trespass:** The enemy often attempts to enter through **"Default Consent."** He looks for a gate that has been left "unlocked" by ignorance, lack of prayer, or unresolved ancestral open doors. If an entity enters without a direct invitation, it is a trespasser, but it will stay until the **Governor of the Estate** (the Mother) serves it with an eviction notice.

### The Mother's Voice as a Key: The Power of Consent

In spiritual law, silence is not neutral; **silence is "Tacit Agreement." The Jurisprudence of Permission:** Because of your unique spiritual "rank" as a mother, your voice has the power to bind and loose over your seed. If you see a pattern of infirmity or a "spirit of lack" trying to land on your children and you say nothing, the spirit world interprets that silence as **"Legal Consent." Activating the Shut Down:** You must use your voice to explicitly **"Withdraw Consent."** You are telling the spirit realm: *"I have reviewed the files of this lineage, and I hereby rescind any permission conscious or unconscious that was given to this pattern. I do not consent to this infirmity!"*

### The Watchman's Duty: Declaring the "No-Fly Zone"

A Watchman is not just someone who "looks"; a Watchman is someone who **"Issues Orders"** based on what they see.

**The Spiritual Injunction:** When you "Shut the Door," you are issuing a **Temporary Restraining Order (TRO)** in the spirit. You are making it "legally impossible" for an entity to operate.

**The "No Fly Zone":** You have the authority to decree a "No Fly Zone" over your husband's health and your children's minds. This means you are telling the enemy: *"You have no landing rights here. Your* *'aircraft' (thoughts of depression, seeds of sickness) cannot enter this airspace. This territory is under the jurisdiction of the King, and the Gate is* ***Locked.****"*

**Isaiah 22:22**

"The key of the house of David I will lay on his shoulder; so he shall open, and no one shall shut; and he shall shut, and no one shall open."

**The Judicial Link:** This is the **"Statute of the Master Key."**
**The "Shoulder" Authority:** Authority is carried on the shoulder (the place of government). You carry the "Government of the Home."
**The "Shut and No One Shall Open" Clause:** This is a **Sovereign Lock**. Once you, as the Mother at the Gate, use the Key of the Word to "Shut" a door against an ancestral spirit, no demonic entity has the legal standing to "pick the lock."
**The Verdict:** You are telling the Court: *"I invoke the Isaiah 22:22 Key! I take the Key of David and I SHUT the gate against every spirit of infirmity and lack! I decree that what I shut today, no demon can open! I withdraw all 'Legal Consent' from ancestral patterns! This gate is* ***Closed,*** *the lock is SEALED, and the 'No-Fly Zone' is active!"*

**The watchman's "Gate-Closing" Decree**

"I strike the Gavel and **I Take my Position** at the Gate of my home! I invoke Isaiah 22:22 and I declare that I hold the 'Key of David' over my husband and my children!

"I hereby 'Rescind' and 'Void' every silent consent! I declare to the spirit world: **Silence Is Broken! I Do Not** consent to the spirit of [infirmity/lack/rebellion]! I withdraw every 'Legal Landing Right' from every ancestral spirit that has tried to claim a foothold in my seed!

"I decree a 'No-Fly Zone' over my children's minds and my husband's vitality! I 'Shut the Door' and I command the lock to be **Sealed** by the Blood of the Lamb! I decree that what I have shut, no demon can open! Every 'Illegal Trespasser' is hereby **Evicted**!

This territory is **Secure**, the Gate is **Watched,** and the King is our Defense! In Jesus' Name!"

### Opening the Gates of Virtue

Being a Gatekeeper is not just about keeping the enemy out; it is about **Authorizing Heaven to Come In**.

**Legislating for Favor:** Just as you can shut doors against darkness, you have the keys to open the doors of "Sudden Opportunity" and "Divine Alignment." You can stand at the gate of your child's future and command the "Gates of Favor" to lift their heads.

**The Protocol of Invitation:** By your prayers, you are the one who signs the "Invitation Letter" for the Holy Spirit to dominate the atmosphere of your home. When the mother is at the gate, the "Climate" of the house changes from one of struggle to one of sovereignty.

To explain **Opening the Gates of Virtue**, we must recognize that the Mother at the Gate is not just a "Border Guard," but a **Kingdom Diplomat**. Your role is to facilitate the "Importation of Glory." In spiritual jurisprudence, Heaven respects the "Law of Invitation." Even though God wants to bless your house, He often waits for the **Authorized Resident** the Mother to open the gate and grant "Legal Entry" to the forces of Favor.

### Legislating for Favor: The Keys of Alignment

Favor is not a random accident; it is a **Judicial Alignment**. It is the "lifting of the heads" of the gates so that the King of Glory can come in with His resources.

**Commanding the "Sudden":** As you stand at the gate of your child's future, you are legislating for **"Divine Synchronicity."** You are decreeing that their path will intersect with the right mentors, the right platforms, and the right opportunities at the exact "Kairos" moment.

**Lifting the Heads:** To command the gates to "lift their heads" means to remove the "Ceilings" of ancestral limitation. You are telling the spirit realm: *"The old height is no longer sufficient! I am opening the High Gates for my seed to walk into 'Sudden Opportunities' that the previous generations could not reach!"*

**The Protocol of Invitation: Signing the "Heavenly Visa"**

In the spirit, the Holy Spirit is a Gentleman He enters where He is **Authorized and Invited**.

**The "Invitation Letter":** Your daily, disciplined prayer is the **"Official Signing"** of the invitation. You are telling the Host of Heaven: *"You have my full permission to dominate the atmosphere of this nursery, this kitchen, and this marriage. I authorize the 'Climate of Zion' to overwrite the 'Climate of the World' in this home."*

**From Struggle to Sovereignty:** When a mother sits at the gate, the household "Weather" changes. The spirit of "Struggle" (constantly fighting to survive) is replaced by the spirit of **"Sovereignty"** (governing from a place of rest). You are moving your home from a "War Zone" to a "Palace of the King."

**Psalm 24:7**

**"Lift up your heads, O you gates! And be lifted up, you everlasting doors! And the King of glory shall come in."**

**The Judicial Link:** This is the **"Statute of the King's Entry."**

**"Lift Up Your Heads":** This is a **Command of Expansion**. It is the Mother at the Gate telling the "circumstances" and "limitations" of the home to make room for a Higher Authority.

**"The King of Glory Shall Come In":** This is the **Result of Authorization**. Once the heads are lifted and the invitation is signed, the "Glory" (the *Kabod* the heavy weight of God's wealth and presence) is legally bound to enter.

**The Verdict:** You are telling the Court: *"I invoke the Psalm 24:7 Mandate! I stand at the gate of my child's [career/education/future] and I command the heads to* ***Lift****! I sign the Invitation Letter for the King of Glory to occupy my household! I decree that every door of 'Sudden Opportunity' is now* ***Open!*** *The King is coming in, and the climate is* ***Changing****! The Gavel is struck; the gates are* ***Lifted****!"*

**The Watchman's "Favor-Opening" Decree**

"I strike the Gavel and **I Take My Position** at the Gate of Invitation! I invoke Psalm 24:7 and I command every gate of my child's future to **Lift Up Its Head**! I decree that the 'Everlasting Doors' of Favor and Divine Alignment are **Swung Wide Now!**

"I hereby 'Sign the Invitation' for the Holy Spirit to dominate every room in this house! I authorize the 'Climate of Zion' to overwrite every frequency of struggle, anxiety, and lack! I decree that the 'Weather' of my home is now Sovereign Peace and Perpetual Surplus!

"I command 'Sudden Opportunities' to find my seed! I decree that they are 'Divinely Aligned' with the movers and shakers of the Kingdom! I open the gates of Wisdom, the gates of Wealth, and the gates of Influence over my lineage! I declare that the King of Glory is coming in with His 'Heavy Weight' of Favor, and **No Man** can shut what I have opened today! The heads are lifted, the King is in, and the Favor is **Mine**! In Jesus' Name!"

**The Seat of the Elder**

**Proverbs 31:23** mentions that a virtuous woman's husband is known in the gates, where he sits among the elders. This is a reflection of the **Mother's Governance**.

**The Invisible Support:** The reason the household thrives at the gate is that the mother has already secured the "Spiritual Perimeter." You are the "Secret Legislator" who handles the legal battles in the spirit so that your family can walk in victory in the natural.

**The Gavel of the Home:** Your kitchen table, your prayer closet, and your bedroom are the "Courtrooms" where you sit as a Governor. When you speak a word of correction or a word of blessing, you are not just giving advice you are **issuing a decree from the Seat of Authority**. **Mathew 16:19** "And I will give you the keys of the kingdom of heaven, and whatever you bind on earth will be bound in heaven, and whatever you loose on earth will be loosed in heaven."

**The Judicial Link:** This is the **"Master Key"** for the Mother at the Gate.

**The Binding (Shutting):** To "bind" is a legal term meaning to forbid or declare unlawful. When you bind addiction or failure in your child, you are telling the Supreme Court of Heaven that this behavior is "Illegal" in your jurisdiction.

**The Loosing (Opening):** To "loose" means to permit or release from a contract. You have the authority to "loose" the hidden stars and the "Touch Not" mandate over your seed.

**The Heavenly Enforcement:** This scripture guarantees that the moment you "lock" a door on earth, the Sheriffs of Heaven arrive to place the seal on it. Heaven does not act until the Gatekeeper on earth speaks.

**The Watchman's Decree for The Gate**

"I strike the Gavel and take my seat at the Gate of my household! I am the Governor of this atmosphere, and I hold the Keys of the Kingdom. In the name of Jesus, I SHUT the gate against every spirit of delay, every marine monitoring spirit, every spirit spouses and every ancestral cycle of pain. I declare your entry is an illegal trespass!

**I Open** the gates of wisdom, knowledge, understanding, fear of God, wealth, and divine health over my seed. I loose the virtues of their destiny and command the 'Ancient Doors' of their greatness to lift up their heads. I decree that my home is a 'Fortress of Light' where only the Kingdom of God has a legal right to legislate. The Gavel has fallen. The Decree is set. The Gate is Secured! In Jesus' Name!"

## Chapter 3: Guarding The Incubation

***Shielding the Womb from Miscarriages, Disorders, and the Theft of Virtues***

In the spirit realm, the womb is not just a biological organ; it is a **Divine Laboratory** and a **Strategic Greenhouse**. Because it is the location where a spirit is being "clothed" with a physical body and a destiny, it is the highest value target for the enemy.

This chapter reveals that a mother must move from being a "carrier" to being a **Security Detail**. You are guarding the "Incubation Phase" the most vulnerable window where the enemy seeks to abort the physical body or, failing that, to "heist" the spiritual virtues before birth.

### Shielding the Physical Temple (Aborting the Abortion)

The enemy often attempts to "terminate the contract" before the child can even enter the earth realm. This manifests as miscarriages or "unexplained" complications that leads to stillbirth, deformity, disability by collecting virtues from the womb.

**The Spirit of Barrenness vs. The Spirit of Life:** Every miscarriage has a spiritual root seeking to deny a "Star" its entry into the earth. You must legislate that your womb is a **"Covenant Zone"** where death has no legal standing.

**The Gavel against Disorders:** Genetic "disorders" are often the enemy's attempt to "vandalize" the temple. By standing over the incubation, you are enforcing the **Original Blueprint**. You are decreeing that every cell, every chromosome, and every organ must align with the "Perfect Image" of God, rejecting any "corrupted data" from the bloodline, from the evil one in the territory.

To explain **Shielding the Physical Temple**, we must view the womb not merely as a biological vessel, but as a **High-Security Construction Site** of the Kingdom. In spiritual jurisprudence, the gestation period is the "Assembly Stage" of a Divine Weapon. The enemy's strategy of "Aborting the Abortion" is a pre-emptive strike intended to "vandalize" or "terminate" the Physical Temple before the spirit can fully occupy its earthly seat.

By standing over the womb as a Governor, you are enforcing **Spiritual Building Codes** that protect the child from the "Looting" of virtues during the incubation process.

**The Spirit of Barrenness vs. The Spirit of Life**

In the spirit, "Barrenness" is not just the inability to conceive; it is a **Judicial Embargo** against the manifestation of a "Star."

**The Covenant Zone:** You are legislating that your womb is **"Extraterritorial Property."** Just as an embassy is governed by the laws of its home country rather than the local land, your womb is governed by the **Laws of Zion**, not the "Ancestral Infirmities" of your bloodline.

**Denying Death's Standing:** You are telling the spirit realm: *"Death is a 'Foreign Entity' here. It has no 'Locus Standi' (right to appear) in this womb. This is a Sanctuary of Life, and any contract of miscarriage is hereby* ***Rejected*** *as a fraudulent filing."*

**The Gavel against Disorders: Enforcing the Original Blueprint**

Genetic disorders and birth complications are often the enemy's attempt to "vandalize" the temple injecting **"Corrupted Data"** into the DNA to limit the child's future capacity.

**The Original Blueprint:** In Heaven, there is a "Perfect Image" for your child a blueprint of their DNA that is free from "Bloodline Glitches."

**The Anti-Vandalism Injunction:** By standing over the incubation, you are acting as the **Quality Control Inspector**. You are decreeing: *"I reject the corrupted data from the territory! I command every chromosome and every organ to align with the 'Original Blueprint' stored in the Volume of the Book! I forbid the 'Vandalization' of this temple; the 'Virtues' of this child are* ***Not*** *for collection!"*

**Psalm 139:15-16**

"My frame was not hidden from You, when I was made in secret, and skillfully wrought in the lowest parts of the earth. Your eyes saw my substance, being yet unformed. And in Your book they all were written, the days fashioned for me, when as yet there were none of them."

**The Judicial Link:** This is the **"Statute of Divine Manufacturing."**

**"Skillfully Wrought":** Refers to "intricate embroidery." It implies that God is the **Lead Architect**. If He is the one "embroidering" the DNA, any "disorder" is an illegal "unauthorized edit."

**"In Your Book They All Were Written":** This is the **Original Spec Sheet**. You have the legal right to demand that the physical body matches the "Written Record" in Heaven.

**The Verdict:** You are telling the Court: *"I invoke the 139:15 Manufacturing Clause! I demand that my child's 'Frame' be skillfully wrought according to the King's design! I 'Squelch' the signal of every genetic defect and every territorial infirmity! I decree that the 'Substance' of this child is **Protected** from the womb to the world! The Blueprint is active, and the Temple is **Secured**!"*

**The Watchman's "Womb-Shield" Decree**

"I strike the Gavel and I declare my womb to be a 'Covenant Zone' and a 'Sanctuary of Life'! I invoke Psalm 139:16 and I decree that my child's substance is being 'Skillfully Wrought' according to the Original Blueprint of Heaven!

"I execute a 'Judicial Injunction' against the spirit of barrenness and the spirit of 'Premature Termination'! I 'Abort the Abortion' and I decree that death has **No Legal Standing** in this incubation! I 'Void' every ancestral contract of miscarriage and I command the 'Spirit of Life' to dominate this environment!

"I stand as a Gavel against all 'Genetic Vandalism'! I command every cell, every chromosome, and every organ to 'Align and Comply' with the Perfect Image of God! I reject the 'Corrupted Data' of the territory and the 'Glitch' of the bloodline! I decree that this temple is 'Incorruptible' and 'Fully Functioning'!

"I forbid the enemy from 'Collecting Virtues' from this womb! This child shall be born Whole, Strong, and Spiritually Loaded! The blueprint is sealed, the temple is shielded, and the Life of God is our guarantee! In Jesus' Name!"

**Protecting the Virtues: The Anti Heist Protocol**

The most dangerous attack is not against the body, but against the **Virtues** (the child's inner greatness).

**The Theft of Stars:** In the spirit, a child's destiny can be "exchanged" or "dimmed" while in the womb. This is the "Marine Exchange" where a child born to be a king is spiritually swapped with a spirit of a servant. **Ecclesiastes 10:5-7** "There is an evil I have seen under the sun, the sort of error that arises from a ruler: Folly is set in many high positions, while the rich sit in low ones. I have seen servants on horses, while princes go on foot like servants."

**The Invisible Shield:** As the Watchman, you must "Seal the Womb" with the Fire of the Holy Ghost. You are creating a **Spiritual Lead Lining** around the baby that prevents monitoring spirits from "scanning" the child's destiny or stealing their "Star."

**Today Social Media Era:** Bible says my people are perishing due to lack of knowledge **Hosea 4:6 .** Parents who are Ignorant about the spiritual realm, they have risked the life of their unborn, by posting pregnancy on social media by posting young babies on social media this has led to sometimes death of both mother and a Child during delivery. That is life being harvested prematurely for satanic sacrifice.

To explain the **"Anti-Heist Protocol,"** we must recognize that the enemy is a **Spiritual Pickpocket** who targets "High Value Targets" before they can defend themselves. In the Kingdom, a "Star" is the spiritual signature of a child's authority. If the enemy cannot kill the child, he will attempt a **"Identity Swap,"** trying to steal the "Prince's Horse" and leave the child walking on foot in their own destiny.

**The Theft of Stars: The "Marine Exchange"**

Ecclesiastes 10:5-7 describes a "Spiritual Error" a legal glitch where the **Wrong Spirit** is sitting in the **Right Position**.

**The Spiritual Swap:** This is the "Marine Exchange," where monitoring spirits attempt to "Switch the Frequency" of the child in the womb. They try to take the "Leader's Virtue" and replace it with a "Servant's Spirit" (the spirit of struggle, mediocrity, and "barely getting by").

**The Prince on Foot:** When this heist is successful, the child grows up with the *potential* of a King but the *reality* of a slave. They are always "almost" successful but never "reigning." You must legislate to **Lock the Identity** so no swap can occur.

**The Invisible Shield: The "Lead Lining" Protocol**

In the natural world, lead prevents X-rays from penetrating. In the spirit, **Holy Ghost Fire** creates a "Lead Lining" around the womb.

**Anti Scanning Technology:** Monitoring spirits use "Spiritual Scanners" to look into the womb and see the "Brightness" of the child's Star. They scan for future wealth, future prophetic voices, and future leadership.

**The Fire-Seal:** By "Sealing the Womb" with fire, you are making the baby **Spiritually Invisible** to the enemy's radar. You are creating a "Dark Chamber" where the child is "Skillfully Wrought" in secret, far from the reach of demonic "Identity Thieves."

### The Social Media Era: The "Lack of Knowledge" Trap

Hosea 4:6 warns that "My people are destroyed for lack of knowledge." In the 2026 digital era, "Ignorance" has become a lethal vulnerability.

**The Exposure Risk:** When a parent posts ultrasound photos or newborn pictures on public social media without spiritual covering, they are essentially **"Broadcasting the Star"** to every monitoring spirit in the territory.

**The Harvest of the Unborn:** Unsanctified digital exposure acts as a "Summons" for satanic "harvesters" who look for "High Virtue Life" to sacrifice or siphon. Many "complications" during delivery are actually the result of a **"Spiritual Eye"** that was invited to look at the child through an unprotected screen. As a Watchman, you must treat your pregnancy and your newborn's image as **"Classified Kingdom Data."**

**Hosea 4:6 & Ecclesiastes 10:7**

"My people are destroyed for lack of knowledge... I have seen servants on horses, while princes go on foot like servants."

**The Judicial Link:** This is the **"Statute of Proprietary Privacy."**

**The "Error" Clause:** Ecclesiastes identifies the swap as an "error" that arises from a **Ruler**. As the "Ruler" of your home, if you are ignorant (lack of knowledge), you authorize the "Error."

**The "Lack of Knowledge" Penalty:** The penalty for spiritual exposure is "Destruction." You are telling the Court: *"I repent for any 'Digital Exposure' that invited the enemy to scan my seed! I revoke the 'Public View' of my child's destiny! I invoke the 'Privacy Act of Zion' and I demand that my child stay on their 'Horse' and the servant stay on the ground!"*

**The Verdict:** You are decreeing: *"I move my child from 'Public Information' to 'Top Secret'! I activate the Fire Shield! I forbid any Marine Exchange! My child shall NOT walk while a servant rides! The Star is **Hidden** in the Fire, and the identity is **Locked**!"*

### The Watchman's "Anti-Heist" Decree

"I strike the Gavel and I activate the 'Anti-Heist Protocol' over my seed! I invoke Hosea 4:6 and I decree that I am a **Knowledgeable** Watchman! I repent for every act of 'Digital Exposure' that allowed the enemy to scan my womb!

"I 'Seal the Womb' with the Fire of the Holy Ghost! I decree a 'Spiritual Lead Lining' around my baby! I command every monitoring spirit and every 'Marine Scanner' to go **Blind**! I decree that my child's Star is Invisible to the kingdom of darkness!

"I forbid the 'Marine Exchange'! I invoke Ecclesiastes 10:7 and I decree that my child is a **Prince/Princess** and they shall **Ride** Upon The Horse of their destiny! I forbid any spirit of a servant from swapping places with my seed!

"I cancel every 'Harvest' and every 'Sacrifice' targeting my delivery! I decree that the 'Delivery Room' is a 'No-Fly Zone' for the harvesters of darkness! My child's virtue is **Not** for sale, **Not** for swap, and **Not** for siphoning! The Star is secured, the Prince is mounted, and the Knowledge of God is my Shield! In Jesus' Name!"

### The Law of the "Sanctified Greenhouse"

Just as a greenhouse protects delicate plants from the harsh outside climate, your prayer life creates a **Micro Climate** for the baby.

**Filtering the Environment:** You are guarding against the "Climate of the Lineage." If the family line is prone to depression or "bad luck," you must ensure that climate does not penetrate the "Greenhouse" of your womb.

**The Infusion of Strength:** During incubation, you are not just "waiting"; you are **infusing**. You are speaking strength into the child's bones and wisdom into their spirit. **Exodus 23:26** "No one shall suffer miscarriage or be barren in your land; I will fulfill the number of your days."

**The Judicial Link:** This is the **"Constitutional Guarantee"** for the womb.

**The Territorial Clause:** God refers to "your land." In this mandate, **your womb is your land**. This is a legal promise that within your jurisdiction, "miscarriage" is an illegal intruder.

**The Fulfillment Mandate:** "I will fulfill the number of your days" is a judicial decree that the child has a **Legal Right to Full Term**. Any attempt to end the pregnancy early or to birth a "disordered" destiny is a violation of this Heavenly Statute. You are enforcing the right of the child to arrive "On Time" and "Intact."

### The Watchman's Decree For Incubation

"I strike the Gavel and declare my womb a 'Forbidden Zone' to the kingdom of darkness! I invoke the Covenant of Exodus 23:26 and decree that no miscarriage, no premature birth, and no infirmity can cross this threshold. I declare a 'Spiritual Lockdown' over this incubation!

I forbid any 'Marine Exchange' or 'Theft of Virtues.' I encrypt my child's destiny with the Blood of Jesus it cannot be scanned, it cannot be traded, and it cannot be dimmed. I speak to the DNA and the chromosomes: **Align** with the Perfect Image of Christ! I reject every ancestral disorder and bloodline defect. This child shall be born with their 'Star' intact and their purpose preserved. The number of their days shall be fulfilled in power! In Jesus' Name!"

# Chapter 4: The Labor of Prayer

## *Birthing the Destiny of Your Children through Spiritual Travail*

In the natural, birth is preceded by labor, a period of intense pressure, rhythmic contractions, and agonizing effort. In the spirit, the same principle applies. There are certain dimensions of your child's destiny that cannot be accessed through "casual prayer." They require **Spiritual Travail.**

This chapter reveals that the "Watchman Mother" must sometimes enter the "Delivery Room of the Spirit" to push a destiny out of the heavens and into the earth.

### The Mechanics of Spiritual Travail

Spiritual travail is a deep, agonizing form of intercession where your spirit groans in alignment with the Holy Spirit. It is the "labor pains" of the soul.

**The "Push" Factor:** Just as a physical mother must push to move the baby through the birth canal, the praying mother must "push" through spiritual resistance. Some destinies are "stuck" in the birth canal of the spirit, delayed by ancestral altars or legal claims. Travail is the force that breaks the "water" of stagnation.

**The Rhythmic Contention:** Labor comes in waves. In prayer, you will feel "burden cycles." These are not times to be depressed; they are "Spiritual Contractions." God is signaling that it is time to legislate for a specific breakthrough.

In the spirit realm, **Travail** is the biological equivalent of **Birthing a Reality**. It is a "High Pressure" state where your spirit becomes the womb for a divine mandate. This is not "casual" prayer; it is **Spiritual Obstetrics**.

When you travail, you are acting as the **Authorized Vessel** that bridges the gap between the "Written Decree" in Heaven and its

"Physical Manifestation" on Earth. You are literally **contracting** the spirit world until the physical world is forced to yield.

### The "Push" Factor: Breaking the Stagnation

In natural labor, if the "Push" isn't strong enough, the baby remains in the birth canal, risking oxygen deprivation or death. This is exactly how many destinies are "Stuck" in the spirit.

**The Spiritual Birth Canal:** This is the "Space Between", between the prophecy and the performance. Destinies get stuck here due to **Ancestral Altars** or **Legal Claims** that act as "blockages" or "constrictions" in the canal.

**Breaking the Water of Stagnation:** Travail provides the **Judicial Pressure** required to move a destiny through the "narrow place." When you "Push" in prayer, you are using the force of the Holy Spirit to flush out the blockages. You are decreeing: *"This mandate will not be stillborn! I am pushing until the environment of my lineage is forced to release the star!"*

### The Rhythmic Contention: Understanding Spiritual Contractions

Labor is defined by **Waves**. If a mother doesn't understand contractions, she will mistake the pain for "internal injury." Similarly, if a Watchman doesn't understand "Burden Cycles," they will mistake them for depression or spiritual burnout.

**Spiritual Contractions:** These are sudden, intense "Grips" on your spirit. You may feel a heavy burden for your child or husband out of nowhere. This is not the time to weep in despair; it is the time to **Legislate**. The "Contraction" is God's signal that the "Cervix of the Spirit" is opening.

**Frequency and Intensity:** As the "Delivery Date" of a breakthrough nears, these burdens will become more frequent and more intense. This is the **Rhythmic Contention** you are contending with the resistance of the old season to give birth to the new.

**Galatians 4:19**

"My little children, for whom I labor in birth again until Christ is formed in you..."

**The Judicial Link:** This is the **"Statute of the Formational Labor."**

**The "Labor in Birth Again":** This refers to **Birth Pangs**. Paul is saying that the "Formation" of Christ in the seed requires a "Labor" from the Governor.

**The "Until" Clause:** This proves that travail is **Goal Oriented**. It does not stop because you are tired; it stops **UNTIL** the formation is complete.

**The Verdict:** You are telling the Court: *"I invoke the Galatians 4:19 Protocol! I enter into 'Spiritual Travail' for my seed! I recognize these 'Burden Cycles' as Divine Contractions! I refuse to be depressed; I choose to be Productive! I am 'Pushing' through the birth canal of this lineage until the Christ Identity is fully formed and manifest! The stagnation is broken; the 'Push' is active!"*

**The Watchman's Travail Decree**

"I strike the Gavel and I enter into the 'Mechanics of Spiritual Travail'! I invoke Galatians 4:19 and I decree that I am 'Laboring' until the full destiny of my seed is birthed into this realm!

"I activate the 'Push Factor'! I command every 'Stuck' destiny in my bloodline to **Move**! I 'Break the Water' of stagnation and I command every ancestral altar and every legal claim that is constricting the birth canal to **Shatter** by the Fire of the Ghost!

"I recognize my 'Burden Cycles' as 'Spiritual Contractions'! I refuse the spirit of depression and I put on the Mantle of the Intercessor! I 'Contend' in this wave until the 'Cervix of the Spirit' is fully dilated! I decree that there shall be no stillbirth, no delay, and no complications in the delivery of this mandate!

"I am 'Pushing' until the Star is visible! I am 'Laboring' until the King is manifest! The pressure is increasing, the breakthrough is near, and the Gavel has fallen! **Birth Is Imminent!** In Jesus' Name!"

### Breaking the "Stuck" Destiny

Many children are "spiritually breached" they are coming into the world or their purpose the wrong way, leading to struggle and confusion.

**The Midwife of the Spirit:** As a mother, you act as the Midwife. Your travail "repositions" the child in the spirit. When you groan in prayer, you are adjusting the spiritual alignment of your child's career, marriage, and character.

**Forceful Entry:** The Kingdom of Heaven suffers violence, and the violent take it by force (Matthew 11:12). Travail is the "Holy Violence" required to ensure that your child is not "stillborn" in their purpose.

To explain **Breaking the "Stuck" Destiny**, we must recognize that in the spirit, as in the natural, the "Position" of the child determines the "Ease" of the delivery. A "Spiritually Breached" child is one whose destiny is misaligned they are gifted but lack character, or they have a mandate but are in the wrong geography.

When a destiny is "Stuck," it creates a state of **Stagnation and Suffocation**. As the Governor of your home, you must step into the judicial role of the **Spiritual Midwife** to force a realignment and ensure a "Forceful Entry" into the earth realm.

### The Midwife of the Spirit: The Power of Repositioning

In a natural birth, a "breached" baby (coming feet-first) is a medical emergency that can lead to death or trauma. Spiritually, a breach occurs when a child tries to enter their purpose through the "wrong door" or at the "wrong frequency."

**The Adjustment of Groans:** The Bible says the Spirit helps our infirmities with "groanings which cannot be uttered" (Romans

8:26). These groans are **Spiritual Manipulations.** Just as a midwife uses her hands to turn a baby in the womb, your "Travail" uses spiritual pressure to **reposition** your child.

**Aligning the Future:** Your prayer "turns" the child so they enter their career, their marriage, and their character building years "Head First" with clarity, vision, and the right mental posture. You are decreeing: *"I refuse to let my child enter their purpose 'sideways'! I am repositioning their heart until it aligns with the North Star of Zion!"*

**Forceful Entry: The "Holy Violence" of Delivery**

There are some demonic structures ancestral altars or territorial principalities that will never "voluntarily" release a child. They intend for the purpose to be **"Stillborn"** (dead on arrival).

**The Matthew 11:12 Mandate:** "The kingdom of heaven suffers violence, and the violent take it by force." In the context of the Mother at the Gate, this "Violence" is the **Intensity of Intercession.**

**The Pressure of Victory:** Travail is the "Holy Violence" that creates an environment so pressurized that the enemy *cannot hold* the child anymore. You are not "asking" the birth canal to open; you are **forcing** it to expand by the power of the Ghost.

**Micah 4:10**

"Be in pain, and labor to bring forth, O daughter of Zion, like a woman in birth pangs. For now you shall go forth from the city, you shall dwell in the field, and to Babylon you shall go. There you shall be delivered; there the Lord will redeem you from the hand of your enemies."

**The Judicial Link:** This is the **"Statute of the Forced Deliverance."**

**"Be in Pain and Labor":** This means to "twist," "" or "dance in pain." It describes the **Violent Agitation** of prayer that breaks spiritual resistance.

**"There You Shall Be Delivered":** This is a **Geographical and Spiritual Guarantee**. It implies that even if the child is in "Babylon" (a place of captivity or confusion), the labor of the "Daughter of Zion" (the Mother) will force the "Redemption" to occur.

**The Verdict:** You are telling the Court: *"I invoke the Micah 4:10 Mandate! I am in 'Holy Agitation' for my seed! I recognize that my child is 'Stuck,' and I refuse to accept a stillbirth! I act as the Midwife and I command a 'Repositioning' now! I use the 'Holy Violence' of the Spirit to force a delivery from the hand of the enemy! Babylon must release them! The birth canal must yield! The Star is coming out* ***Now****!"*

### The Watchman's "Midwife" Decree

"I strike the Gavel and I take my place as the 'Midwife of the Spirit' over my lineage! I invoke Micah 4:10 and I enter into the 'Holy Agitation' required to bring forth my child's destiny!

"I command a **'repositioning'** of every spiritually breached area of my child's life! I decree that their career, their marriage, and their character are being aligned with the Original Blueprint! I 'Turn' them in the spirit from confusion to clarity, from feet- first to head-first!

"I execute the 'Holy Violence' of Matthew 11:12! I decree that the Kingdom of Heaven in my home suffers violence, and I am **Taking** my child's breakthrough **By Force**! I break the grip of every ancestral altar that is trying to cause a stillbirth! I command the 'Water of Stagnation' to break and the 'Birth Canal of Purpose' to **Open Wide**!

"I decree 'Forced Deliverance' from every Babylonian system! My child shall not be 'Stuck'; they shall be 'Released'! They shall not be 'Delayed'; they shall 'Manifest'! The Gavel has fallen, the Midwife has spoken, and the **Destiny Is Out**! In Jesus' Name!"

**Moving from Conception to Manifestation**

It is possible to "conceive" a great word from God about your child but never "birth" it.

**The Danger of Miscarrying Purpose:** Many mothers have "prophetic pregnancies" that never reach delivery because they stopped praying once the child was born physically.

**The Final Push:** This chapter teaches you how to stay in the "Delivery Room" until you see the physical manifestation of the promise. You don't stop when they graduate; you stop when they are fully established in the throne God assigned to them. **Isaiah 66:8**

"Who has heard such a thing? Who has seen such things? Shall the earth be made to give birth in one day? Or shall a nation be born at once? For as soon as Zion travailed, she gave birth to her children."

**The Judicial Link:** This is the **"Statute of Birth"** in the Kingdom.

**The Trigger of Travail:** The scripture is clear: birth is a direct result of *travail.* Without the "Zion cry," the "Nation" (the greatness inside your child) remains locked in the womb of the spirit.

**The Speed of Manifestation:** The verse suggests that travail "accelerates" the process. What should take years of struggle can be "born in one day" when a mother decides to enter the labor of prayer. You are legislating for **Spiritual Acceleration**.

Galatians 4:19 "My little children, for whom I labor in birth again until Christ is formed in you" Paul reveals a mystery here, he is "laboring in birth *again.*"

**Post Physical Labor:** This proves that even after a child is born physically, the mother must perform **"Secondary Labor"** to ensure that the character of Christ is formed in them.

**The Goal of Travail:** You are not just laboring for them to be successful; you are laboring until the "Image of the Son" is fully visible in their lives. This is the ultimate "Touch Not" mandate a child who carries the undeniable image of Christ is untouchable by the enemy.

### The Watchman's Decree for Labor

"I strike the Gavel and enter the Delivery Room of the Spirit! I declare that my seed shall not be 'stuck' in the birth canal of destiny. I invoke Isaiah 66:8 and begin the travail of Zion over my household! I push against every ancestral delay! I push against every demonic blockade! I push against every spirit of stagnation!

I decree that the 'Nation' inside my children is coming forth NOW! I refuse to have a prophetic miscarriage. I will labor in birth until Christ is fully formed in my sons and daughters. I command the 'Ancient Gates' to open and let the King of Glory enter the lives of my seed. It is birthed! It is manifest! It is done! In Jesus' Name!"

## Chapter 5: Raising Lions and Lionesses

***Shifting from "Survival Prayers" to "Throne Room Decrees"***

Most mothers pray from a place of **panic**, but the Watchman Mother prays from a place of **position**. This chapter marks a transition in your spiritual warfare strategy. You are no longer merely asking God to "keep your children safe" or "help them get by." Instead, you are recognizing that you are birthing **Royalty**.

If you view your children as "sheep," you will pray for their protection from wolves. But if you view them as **Lions**, you will pray for their **Territorial Expansion**. This is the shift from "Survival" to "Dominion."

### Dismantling the "Victim" Mentality in Prayer

Survival prayers are reactive. They are born out of a fear of what the enemy might do.

**The Survival Trap:** "Lord, please don't let them do drugs," or "Lord, please let them find a job." These prayers acknowledge the enemy's power more than God's mandate.

**The Throne Room Shift:** You must begin to legislate their **Inheritance**. Instead of praying they "survive" the world, you decree that they will **change** the world. You are not raising children to hide from the dark; you are raising Lions to roar at the dark until it flees.

To dismantle the "Victim Mentality" in prayer, you must understand that **the language of the victim is "Help Me," but the language of the Legislator is "It is Written."** When you pray survival based prayers, you are unintentionally petitioning the Court of Heaven as a refugee rather than a Citizen Governor. Deepening this shift requires a complete overhaul of your spiritual vocabulary and your internal posture.

### The "Frequency of Fear" vs. The "Frequency of Faith"

Survival prayers are often fueled by **Cortisol** (the stress hormone) rather than the **Anointing.**

**The Reactive Trap:** When you pray, "Lord, keep them away from the wrong crowd," your mind is focused on the "wrong crowd." In the spirit, you are inadvertently giving "airtime" to the enemy's plans. You are treating the enemy as a formidable giant and God as a rescue squad.

**The Proactive Shift:** The Throne Room Mother ignores the "wrong crowd" and speaks to the **Magnetism of the Star**. You decree: *"I command the divine pull of destiny to attract destiny helpers into my child's path. I decree their spirit is allergic to the ungodly, and they carry a frequency that repels every agent of darkness."* You aren't asking God to stop a negative; you are **authorizing a positive.**

### Moving from "Petitions" to "Injunction

A petition is a request that can be denied; an **Injunction** is a judicial order that restrains a party from an action.

**The Victim's Petition:** "God, please heal my child's mind." This assumes the sickness has a right to be there and you are begging for a pardon.

**The Legislator's Injunction:** "I move for a Summary Judgment against the spirit of anxiety. I present the Blood of the Covenant as evidence that this child's mind is the 'Property of the Kingdom.' I issue a Restraining Order against the spirit of heaviness. It is legally forbidden from operating within 100 miles of my child's consciousness."

**The Difference:** One waits for a "maybe"; the other **enforces a "must."**

### Raising "Light Bearers" instead of "Darkness Hiders"

The victim mentality prays for a "hedge of protection" so the child can hide safely within it. The Throne Room Mother prays for the child to **BE the Light.**

**The Shift in Strategy:** Lions do not ask the forest for permission to be there. When you legislate their inheritance, you are decreeing that **they are the atmosphere shifters.**

**The Decree:** Instead of "Don't let the world influence them," you decree: *"My child is an Ambassador of the Third Heaven. Everywhere their feet tread, the culture of the Kingdom is established. They do not adapt to the darkness; the darkness adapts to them. They are not the 'Prey' of the world's systems; they are the 'Prophets' to the world's systems."*

**Acknowledging the "Finished Work"**

The ultimate dismantling of the victim mentality is the realization that the battle is already won. Survival prayers act as if the outcome is in doubt. Throne Room decrees act as if the **Verdict is already in.**

**The Gavel of Faith:** You aren't praying *to* get a victory; you are legislating *from* the victory Christ already secured. Your job isn't to defeat the enemy, he's already defeated. Your job is to **enforce his eviction notice** from your child's life.

**Luke 10:19**

"Behold, I give you the authority to trample on serpents and scorpions, and over all the power of the enemy, and nothing shall by any means hurt you."

**The Judicial Link:** This is the "Badge of Office" for every mother. Jesus didn't say He would trample them *for* you; He said He gave **YOU** the authority to do it. The victim waits for God to step in; the Lion Mother steps in *as* God's legal representative on earth.

**The Watchman's Transition Decree**

"I strike the Gavel and officially resign from the position of a 'Survivalist.' I repent for every prayer birthed in fear and every decree that honored the enemy's power. I take my seat in the Throne Room of Christ!

I decree that my children are not 'survivors' of their generation; they are the **Overcomers** of it! I don't pray for them to escape the heat; I decree they are 'Fire Walkers' like Shadrach, Meshach, and Abednego. I authorize their spirits to dominate every environment they enter. I am not raising children to 'just get by'; I am legislating for them to **'Take Over.'** The victim is dead; the Governor has risen! In Jesus' Name!"

### The DNA of the Lion of Judah

Your children carry a "Genetic Royalty" through the Blood of Jesus. A lion does not ask for permission to rule the forest; its presence is its authority.

**Cultivating the Roar:** Your decrees are the "Roar" that trains your children's spirits to take their place. When you speak over them, you are activating their **Leadership DNA**.

**Throne Room Decrees:** These are judicial orders issued from the Third Heaven. You are sitting with Christ in heavenly places (Ephesians 2:6), and from that height, you look down at the "Lions" you are raising and command their "Stars" to align with their "Thrones."

### The Systemic Defense of the Pride

Lions do not hunt or defend alone; they operate in a "Pride." As the Mother, you are establishing a **Systemic Defense**.

**Building a Wall of Sovereignty:** You are decreeing that your household is a "Territory of Judah." In this territory, the laws of the "Jungle" (the world) do not apply.

**The Preservation of Thrones:** Every child has a "Throne" (a place of high level influence) assigned to them. This chapter teaches you how to legislate against "Usurpers" those spirits or people who try to sit on your child's seat of authority "The spirit of Athaliah and Adonaijah" **Genesis 49:9-10** "Judah is a lion's whelp; from the prey, my son, you have gone up. He bows down, he lies down as a lion; and as a lion, who shall rouse him? The scepter shall not depart from Judah, nor a lawgiver from between his feet, until Shiloh comes; and to Him shall be the obedience of the people."

**The Judicial Link:** This is the **"Decree of the Scepter." The Development of the Lion:** Notice the progression: "Lion's whelp" (the child) to "as a lion" (the adult). Jacob, the parent, is legislating the *identity* of his son. He isn't hoping Judah becomes a leader; he is **declaring** it.

**The Permanent Scepter:** The "Scepter" represents the **Mandate of Governance**. By using this scripture, you are decreeing that the "Authority to Rule" shall never depart from your bloodline. You are locking your children into a destiny of leadership that lasts until "Shiloh" (the Messiah) returns.

**The Watchman's Decree for Raising Lions**

"I strike the Gavel and renounce the spirit of survival! I refuse to pray 'begging' prayers over my seed. I take my seat in the Throne Room and I decree: My children are the offspring of the Lion of Judah! I activate the DNA of Royalty within their blood!

I decree that the Scepter of Authority shall never depart from my household. My sons are Lions of Integrity; my daughters are Lionesses of Power. I command the 'Prey' of this world to be under their feet. I forbid them from walking in timidity or fear. I roar over their destinies and declare that they shall occupy the 'High Places' of the earth! No usurper shall sit on their thrones, and no stranger shall eat their inheritance. The Lion has roared who can but prophesy? In Jesus' Name!"

## Chapter 6: Uprooting The Unwanted Seed

### *Extracting "Normalized Evil" Before It Takes Root in Their Character*

In the agricultural laws of the spirit, there is a phenomenon known as the **"Unwanted Seed."** These are traits, patterns, and inclinations that were not planted by God, nor by the parent, but were "sown by the enemy" during a season of spiritual slumber or through the legal gaps in the family bloodline.

This chapter deals with **"Normalized Evil"** those behaviors that your lineage has accepted as "just the way we are" (e.g., "all the men in our family have tempers" or "all the women are prone to anxiety, anger, rage, pride"). As a Watchman, you are called to be a **Spiritual Geneticist**, identifying and extracting these "weeds" before they choke the "Star" of your child's destiny.

### Identifying the "Normalized" Intruder

"Normalized Evil" is dangerous because it is camouflaged as **personality**.

**The Genetic Lie:** The enemy wants you to believe that a child's inclination toward deception, addiction, or depression is simply "part of their DNA."

**The Judicial Truth:** Anything that does not reflect the "Perfect Image of Christ" is a foreign seed. If it didn't come from the Father of Lights, it doesn't have a legal right to stay in the garden of your child's character. You must refuse to call "genetic baggage" a "personality trait."

### The Protocol of Extraction

Uprooting is a violent, intentional act. It requires the mother to go beyond "behavioral correction" and move into **Root Level Legislation**.

**Targeting the Seed:** You don't just prune the leaves (the behavior); you kill the seed (the spiritual source, the root). If you see a seed of rebellion sprouting in your toddler or teenager, you don't just discipline the child; you **evict the spirit** that sowed the seed.

**The Fire of the Holy Ghost:** This chapter teaches you how to use the "Fire" to incinerate the roots of "Normalized Evil." You are decreeing that the soil of your child's soul is **toxic to the enemy's seed**.

To explain the **Protocol of Extraction**, we must look at it through the lens of **Spiritual Forestry**. Most parents focus on "Lumberjacking" chopping down the visible branches of bad behavior. But in the spirit, if the stump remains, the "sap" of the ancestral line will simply cause it to regrow. Extraction is about **total annihilation of the source.**

### Targeting the Seed: The Difference Between Discipline and Deliverance

Discipline (behavioral correction) is for the child; **Deliverance (Root Level Legislation)** is for the spirit behind the behavior.

**The "Fruit" Fallacy:** When a child is rebellious, lazy, or prone to lying, those are the "leaves." If you only address the leaves through yelling or punishment, you are "pruning" the problem, which often makes it grow back thicker.

**The Root Level Warrant:** As a Watchman, you must look at the behavior and ask: *"Is this just immaturity, or is this a 'Seed' from my father's house?"* If you recognize a pattern of "Divorce" or "Addiction" starting as a small seed of "Isolation" or "Obsession," you don't just talk to the child. You go into your prayer closet and **evict the spirit of the lineage** that is trying to use your child's body as its new host. You are telling the spirit: *"You have no legal right to plant your 'data' in this new generation."*

### The Fire of the Holy Ghost: Creating a "Toxic Soil"

The spirit of a child is "Soil." The enemy is looking for fertile ground to plant "Normalized Evil." The Protocol of Extraction involves using the **Fire of the Holy Ghost** to change the "pH balance" of your child's spiritual environment.

**Incinerating the Roots:** Some spiritual roots go deep into the "sub soil" of the subconscious. You cannot reach these with words. You must call down the Fire to travel down the spiritual umbilical cord and incinerate the "taproot" of the curse. This Fire doesn't hurt the child; it consumes the **foreign DNA** of the enemy.

**A High Heat Atmosphere:** By consistently praying in the spirit and making decrees, you create an atmosphere that is "too hot" for demonic seeds to germinate. You are decreeing: *"The soil of my child's soul is toxic to deception, toxic to lust, and toxic to failure. No weaponized seed can survive the heat of this household!"*

**The Judicial Eviction: "Cease and Desist"**

Extraction is not a suggestion; it is a **Judicial Eviction**.

In the natural, an eviction is a violent removal of a tenant who refuses to leave.

In the spirit, you are serving a "Cease and Desist" order to the "Sower of Tares." You are telling the enemy: *"I have identified your seed. I have exposed your root. By the authority of the Gavel, I rip you out by the foundation!" In the name of Jesus.*

**Jeremiah 1:10**

"See, I have this day set you over the nations and over the kingdoms, to root out and to pull down, to destroy and to throw down, to build and to plant."

**The Judicial Link:** This is your **"Work Order."** Notice the order: you must **root out** and **pull down** *before* you can build or plant. If you try to build a "godly character" on top of an "uprooted ancestral seed," the structure will eventually collapse. You are authorized to be a "Destroyer" of evil seeds so that you can be a "Planter" of divine ones.

**The Watchman's Extraction Decree**

"I strike the Gavel and execute the Warrant of Extraction! I refuse to just 'prune' the behavior of my children; I am going for the **Root**! In the name of Jesus, I identify the seed of [Name specific trait, e.g., anger, delay, fear] and I command it to be **Uprooted** by the Fire of God!

I apply the Fire of the Holy Ghost to the spiritual soil of my child's mind and heart. I incinerate every ancestral 'taproot' that was seeking to draw life from my seed. I decree that the soil of this generation is **Toxic** to the enemy! I evict every 'Normalized Evil' that has hidden in our DNA. I pull it down, I throw it down, and I destroy its legal hold! This soil is now prepared for the Seed of the Word! In Jesus' Name!"

**The Law of the "Clean Slate"**

Every generation has the legal right to a "Clean Slate" through the Blood of Jesus.

**Breaking the Cycle:** You are the "Circuit Breaker." When you uproot an unwanted seed, you are ensuring that your child does not have to fight the same giants you fought.

**Replacing the Seed:** Once the unwanted seed is pulled out, you must immediately **sow the Word**. You fill the "void" with the virtues of the Kingdom so there is no room for the enemy to return with "seven spirits more wicked." **Luke 11:24–26.**

**Mathew 15:13**

"But He answered and said, 'Every plant which My heavenly Father has not planted will be uprooted."

**The Judicial Link:** This is the **"Master Warrant for Extraction."**

**The Legal Standard:** This verse provides the ultimate criteria for what is allowed to grow in your child. If God didn't plant it meaning it isn't Love, Joy, Peace, Longsuffering, etc. It is **legally eligible for uprooting.**

**The Divine Mandate:** Jesus doesn't say "might be uprooted" or "should be uprooted." He issues a definitive judicial decree: **"Will be uprooted."** As a mother, you are the one who executes this warrant on earth. You point to the "plant" of infirmity or pride and say, *"Court of Heaven, I identify this as a plant my Father did not sow. I demand its immediate uprooting!"*

**The Watchman's Decree For Uprooting**

"I strike the Gavel and enter the garden of my child's soul! I invoke Matthew 15:13 and declare a 'Search and Seizure' operation over their character. Every plant, every inclination, and every 'Normalized Evil' that my Heavenly Father has not planted is **Uprooted Now** by the Fire of the Holy Ghost!

I decree that the seeds of ancestral anger, the roots of generational poverty, and the weeds of stagnation are incinerated at the source. I forbid the 'Climate of my Lineage' from nurturing any foreign seed in my seed! I declare the soil of my children's hearts is Holy Ground, reserved only for the Fruits of the Spirit. What was 'normal' in my past is now 'illegal' in their future! The roots are out, and the Word is in! In Jesus' Name!"

# Chapter 7: Guarding The Marriage Bed

## *Protecting the Atmosphere of the Home from Intruding Spirits*

In the architecture of spiritual warfare, the marriage bed is not just a piece of furniture; it is an **Altar**. It is the "Inner Sanctum" of the home where two become one, creating the spiritual "climate" that your children breathe every day.

If the altar of the marriage is defiled, cracked, or left unguarded, it creates a **Legal Breach** a hole in the "Strategic Wall" through which intruding spirits enter to harass the entire household. This chapter reveals that to protect the children, you must first secure the "Command Center" of the home: the marriage.

### The Marriage Bed as a "Portal of Atmosphere"

The spiritual state of the marriage determines the "Weather" of the house.

**The Frequency of Oneness:** When a husband and wife are in alignment, they create a **Sovereign Frequency** that acts as a shield.

**The Breach of Discord:** Bitterness, unresolved anger, or "silent wars" in the marriage bed act as an invitation for "Atmospheric Intruders" spirits of heaviness, strife, and rebellion. Your children are "Atmospheric Sponges"; if the marriage bed is a site of spiritual warfare rather than spiritual rest, the children will manifest the stress of that breach in their behavior and health.

To explain the **Portal of Atmosphere**, we must understand that the marriage union is the spiritual "Thermostat" of the home. In the realm of the spirit, your home is an ecosystem, and the marriage bed is the engine that dictates whether that ecosystem is a **Garden of Peace** or a **Desert of Strife**.

**The Frequency of Oneness: The "Sovereign Shield"**

When a husband and wife are in a state of *Echad* (Biblical Oneness), they emit a spiritual frequency that functions as an **Electromagnetic Shield.**

**The Power of Agreement:** This "Oneness" creates a resonant vibration that is incompatible with demonic interference. It is like a high security "Digital Encryption" over the house. When the parents are aligned, the enemy cannot find a "port" to plug into.

**The Protective Canopy:** This frequency extends outward from the marriage bed, creating a "dome" of protection over the children's bedrooms. In this atmosphere, children thrive, their spirits are at rest, and their "Stars" can shine without the "haze" of parental conflict.

**The Breach of Discord: The "Atmospheric Invitation"**

Discord is not just an emotional issue; it is a **Legal Opening**. When there is unresolved anger or "silent wars" (passive aggressiveness), you are effectively lowering the spiritual "drawbridge" of your fortress.

**Atmospheric Intruders:** Spirits of **Heaviness** (depression), **Strife** (constant arguing), and **Rebellion** do not always enter through the child; they often enter through the "Breach" in the marriage bed. They are attracted to the "scent" of division.

**Children as "Atmospheric Sponges":** Children are spiritually "porous." They absorb the chemical and spiritual data of their environment. If the marriage bed is a place of tension, the children will "wick" that tension into their own spirits. What parents call "behavioral issues" or "nightmares" are often just the child reacting to the **Polluted Weather** created by a fractured union.

**The Portal of Rest vs. The Portal of War**

Your bed is meant to be a **Portal of Rest** (Hebrews 4), where the Presence of God settles. If it becomes a Portal of War, the house becomes "Spiritually Humid" heavy, sticky, and difficult to breathe in.

**The Watchman's Restoration:** To protect the seed, the Mother must legislate the "sanitizing" of this portal. You must decree that the "air" of your marriage is purified so that your children are not forced to breathe the "smog" of discord.

**Amos 3:3**

**"Can two walk together, unless they are agreed?"**

**The Judicial Link:** In the original Hebrew, "agreed" means to meet at an appointed place, to engage, or to be set together by appointment.

**The Legal Requirement for Presence:** God's "Walking" (His manifest Presence and Protection) in your home is legally contingent upon the **Agreement** of the two.

**The Verdict:** If the "two" are not walking in agreement, the "third" (the Holy Spirit) does not have a legal "platform" to stand on to defend the home. Agreement is the **Legal Contract** that keeps the Portal of Atmosphere open to Heaven and closed to Hell.

### The Watchman's Atmospheric Decree

"I strike the Gavel and declare a 'Climate Change' over my home! I repent for every breach of discord, every silent war, and every word of bitterness that has polluted our atmosphere. I invoke Amos 3:3 and decree that my husband and I are in a state of Sovereign Agreement!

I seal the 'Portal of the Marriage Bed' with the Blood of Jesus. I decree that our union is a 'Frequency of Peace' that acts as a shield for our children. I forbid the spirits of heaviness and rebellion from feeding on the vapors of discord. I command the 'Weather' of this house to be Light, Joy, and Rest! My children shall breathe the pure air of the Kingdom! In Jesus' Name!"

### Legislating Against "Intruding Spirits"

There are specific spirits that target the marriage bed to gain access to the seed.

**The Spirit of Strange Altars:** This includes the influence of "past altars" (former relationships or ancestral patterns of infidelity) that try to claim a seat at your current marriage table.

**The Monitoring Spirit:** These entities watch the intimacy of the marriage to find "legal gaps." They look for moments of disconnection to plant seeds of "Foreign Affection" or "Isolation."

**The Watchman's Duty:** As the Mother and Wife, you have the legislative right to **Seal the Room**. You must treat your bedroom as a "Consecrated Courtroom" where no unauthorized entity, physical or spiritual, is permitted to testify.

To deepen the revelation of **Legislating Against Intruding Spirits**, we must shift from a defensive posture to a **Judicial Enforcement** posture. In the spirit, your marriage bed is not just a place of rest; it is a **Subpoena Proof Chamber.** When you legislate, you are issuing a court order that terminates the surveillance and influence of external entities.

### The Spirit of Strange Altars: Terminating Ancient Claims

A "Strange Altar" is any spiritual foundation built on a "Contract of the Past." This includes "Soul Ties" from former relationships or "Ancestral Covenants" of infidelity that exist in the bloodline.

**The Claim to the Table:** These spirits attempt to "sit at your table" by citing old legal grounds. They argue that because "infidelity" or "rejection" was a law in your father's house, it has a right to be a law in yours.

**The Judicial Severing:** To legislate is to present a **"Certificate of Divorce"** from every past altar. You are declaring that the "New Covenant" in Christ has bought out the "Title Deed" of your marriage. You are not just asking these spirits to leave; you are proving they no longer have a legal "Lease" on your intimacy.

**The Monitoring Spirit: Closing the "Legal Gaps"**

Monitoring spirits are "Spiritual Intelligence Agents." Their job is to find a **"Crack in the Wall"**, a moment of unresolved silence, a night spent sleeping back to back in anger, or a secret resentment.

**Seeds of Foreign Affection:** They don't usually attack with a hammer; they attack with a "Seed." They look for a gap in the marriage bed to plant "Foreign Affection" (emotional affairs) or "Isolation" (spiritual withdrawal).

**The Security Protocol:** Legislating against these agents means you are **"Scrambling their Signal."** By the Blood of Jesus, you create a "Spiritual Stealth Mode" over your bedroom. You decree that your intimacy is "Classified Data" that no monitoring spirit has the "Security Clearance" to access.

**The Watchman's Duty: The Consecrated Courtroom**

As the Mother and Wife, you hold the **Gavel of the Household**. You must treat your bedroom as a **"Sanctuary of Sovereignty."**

**The No Testimony Rule:** In a courtroom, a judge can strike a testimony from the record. If the enemy tries to "testify" to your husband about your flaws, or "testify" to you about his failures, you must **Sustain an Objection** in the spirit.

**Sealing the Room:** You are not just locking the door; you are "Sealing the Portal." You are decreeing that the only "Witness" allowed in that room is the Holy Spirit.

**Mathew 19:6**

"So then, they are no longer two but one flesh. Therefore, what God has joined together, let not man or spirit separate."

**The Judicial Link:** This is the **"Supreme Court Ruling"** on Marriage.

**The "Joined Together" Clause:** The "together " means to "yoke together" or "fasten." It is a legal binding performed by God Himself.
**The Injunction:** "Let not man separate" is a **Divine Injunction**. In the original language, it is a command: *"Stop the separation!"*
**The Verdict:** This verse gives you the authority to tell every "Strange Altar" and "Monitoring Spirit": *"You are attempting to interfere with a Divine Yoking. You are in Contempt of the Supreme Court of Heaven. I enforce the 'Let Not Separate' decree over this bed!"*

### The Watchman's Legislative Decree

"I strike the Gavel and take my seat in the Courtroom of my home! I invoke Matthew 19:6 and declare that what God has yoked, no spirit shall separate! I issue a 'Summary Judgment' against every 'Strange Altar' seeking to speak from my past or my husband's lineage. I declare those ancient contracts **Null And Void** by the Blood of Jesus!

I blind every 'Monitoring Spirit' and dismantle every 'Listening Post' the enemy has tried to set up in our bedroom. I decree that our intimacy is a 'Classified Kingdom Secret'! I forbid the spirits of isolation and foreign affection from finding a gap in our union. I seal this room as a 'Consecrated Courtroom' where only the testimony of the Holy Spirit is permitted! The decree is final. The wall is secure. In Jesus' Name!"

### Guarding the "Bed Undefiled"

The "Undefiled Bed" is a legal status in the spirit. It means the altar is clean, the "Title Deed" is clear, and the Presence of God is the primary resident.
**Sanitizing the Sanctuary:** This chapter teaches you how to "mop" the atmosphere of your bedroom with the Blood of Jesus. You are removing the "scent" of old arguments and the "residue" of outside pressures.

**Protecting the Seed through the Union:** When the marriage bed is guarded, the children sleep under a "Closed Heaven." The security of the parents' union provides the "Spiritual Canopy" that prevents nightmares and night terrors from attacking the children.

**Hebrews 13:4**

"Marriage is honorable among all, and the bed undefiled; but fornicators and adulterers God will judge."

**The Judicial Link:** This is the **"Statute of the Altar."**

**The "Honorable" Clause:** The word "honorable" means precious, of great price, and held in honor. By keeping the bed "undefiled," you are maintaining a **High Value Security Clearance** in the spirit.

**The Judicial Protection:** The verse ends with a promise of "Judgment" against intruders. When you keep your marriage bed consecrated, you authorize God to act as a **Judicial Bodyguard** over your union. You are telling the spirit world: *"This altar is Undefiled. Therefore, any spirit of lust, strife, divorce or separation that touches this bed is subject to immediate Divine Judgment!"*

**The Watchman's Decree For The Marriage Bed**

"I strike the Gavel and declare the Marriage Bed of this house a 'Consecrated Altar'! I invoke Hebrews 13:4 and decree that our union is honorable and our bed is undefiled. I apply the Blood of Jesus to the four corners of our bedroom and the atmosphere of our intimacy!

I issue a 'Restraining Order' against every intruding spirit of strife, coldness, and strange fire. I forbid any 'Monitoring Spirit' from observing our union or finding a breach in our wall. I decree that the climate of our marriage is PEACE, and this peace shall flow out as a canopy over my children. I shut the door against ancestral patterns of divorce and betrayal! Our bed is a Sanctuary of Light, and our union is a Fortress for our seed! In Jesus' Name!"

# Chapter 8: Bloodline Sanitation

## *Scrubbing Corrupted Foundations from Both Maternal and Paternal Lineages*

In the spirit realm, every child is the "Joint Property" of two distinct bloodlines. While we celebrate the physical heritage, we must acknowledge that blood carries **Data** both the blessings of the righteous and the "Corrupted Files" of the ancestors.

**Bloodline Sanitation** is the judicial process of "scrubbing" the spiritual conduit of your child's inheritance. It is not enough to clean your side of the family; as the Watchman, you must stand at the intersection of both lineages and apply the **Solvent of the Blood of Jesus** to dissolve every legal claim, every recurring infirmity, and every pattern of failure coming from either side.

### The Concept of "Spiritual Data" in the Blood

Science tells us that DNA carries physical traits, but Scripture reveals that blood carries the **Voice of History**.

**The Paternal and Maternal Records:** Your child is the "convergence point" of two histories. If there is a pattern of "premature death" on the father's side and "depression" on the mother's side, those two "files" are seeking to merge in your child's life.

**The Scrubbing Protocol:** Sanitation is the act of "deleting" the corrupted files. You are not "disowning" your family; you are **sanitizing the inheritance**. You are telling the spirit world: *"The blood flowing through this child is being filtered. I authorize the transfer of the virtues, but I veto the transfer of the vices."*

### Scrubbing the "Corrupted Foundations"

Psalm 11:3 asks, *"If the foundations are destroyed, what can the righteous do?"* Many children struggle not because of their own choices, but because the "Soil" they were planted in (their lineage) is contaminated.

**The Ancestral Lien:** A "Lien" is a legal right to keep possession of property belonging to another person until a debt is discharged. The enemy often places a "Lien" on a child's destiny based on a "Debt" (sin or covenant) incurred by a grandfather or great grandmother.

**The Blood Solvent:** The Blood of Jesus is the only legal substance capable of "dissolving" a spiritual lien. When you "scrub" the bloodline, you are presenting a **"Paid in Full"** receipt to the enemy, forcing him to release his grip on your child's health, mind, and finances.

To explain **Scrubbing the Corrupted Foundations**, we must understand that in the spirit, your child is "Real Estate." If that real estate was inherited with a "Spiritual Lien," the enemy acts as a predatory debt collector, claiming he has a legal right to occupy the child's health, peace, or finances because of a "debt" incurred by an ancestor.

**The Ancestral Lien: The Debt of the Fathers**

In natural law, a **Lien** is a legal claim against an asset. In spiritual law, a lien is established when an ancestor enters into an unholy covenant, commits a "land defiling" sin, or leaves a "spiritual debt" (unconfessed iniquity) unpaid.

**The Claim on the Destiny:** The enemy argues in the Court of Heaven: *"I have a right to this child's mind (Autism, schizophrenia) because their great grandfather gave me the 'Title Deed' through his occult practices,"* or *"I have a right to this child's womb because of the blood shed in the previous generation."*

**The Silent Occupier:** This is why some children experience "unexplained" delay or "inherited" sickness. They are living on a foundation that has a **Foreclosure Notice** from the kingdom of darkness.

**The Blood Solvent: The Divine "Quiet Title" Action**

In law, a "Quiet Title" action is a lawsuit intended to establish a party's title to real property against anyone and everyone, effectively "quieting" any challenges or claims. **The Blood of Jesus is your "Quiet Title" Solvent.**

**Dissolving the Debt:** The Blood is not just a liquid; it is a **Legal Currency**. It doesn't just "cover" the debt; it *dissolves* the legal standing of the creditor.

**The "Paid in Full" Receipt:** When you apply the Blood to the foundations of the maternal and paternal lines, you are presenting a **Receipt from the Cross** that proves the debt was discharged 2,000 years ago. You are telling the enemy: *"Your lien is no longer enforceable. The debt was settled by the Son, and I am here to enforce the discharge papers!"*

**Scrubbing the Soil**

If the "Soil" of the lineage is contaminated with the chemicals of ancestral sin, the child's "Star" cannot take root. Scrubbing the foundation means you are **Decontaminating the Earth** of your child's history. You are washing away the "residue" of the past so the "Seed" of the child's future can grow in Holy Ground.

**Colossians 2:14**

"Having wiped out the handwriting of requirements that was against us, which was contrary to us. And He has taken it out of the way, having nailed it to the cross."

**The Judicial Link:** This is the **"Master Statute of Debt Cancellation."**

**The Handwriting of Requirements:** This refers to the **"Legal Ledger"** of your bloodline, the record of every ancestral "contract" or "lien."

**The Wiping Out:** The "wiped out" means to erase, to smear over, or to **totally obliterate a record**.

**The Verdict:** This verse proves that the Blood of Jesus "scrubs" the record clean. It doesn't just hide the ancestral debt; it **removes the ink**. When you legislate from this verse, you are telling the

Court: *"There is no longer any 'Handwriting' that can be used against my child. The record has been scrubbed! The foundation is clear!"*

**The Watchman's Foundational Scrubbing Decree**

"I strike the Gavel over the maternal and paternal foundations of my seed! I invoke Colossians 2:14 and declare that every 'Handwriting of Requirements' every ancestral lien, every demonic debt, and every satanic contract is WIPED OUT by the Blood of Jesus!

I apply the 'Blood Solvent' to the roots of my child's lineage. I dissolve every legal claim the enemy holds over their mind, their body, and their future. I present the 'Paid in Full' receipt of the Cross! I decree that the soil of this generation is now **Decontaminated**. I 'Quiet the Title' of my child's destiny; no stranger has a claim, and no creditor has a voice! The foundation is Holy, the debt is canceled, and my seed is FREE! In Jesus' Name!"

**Standing as the "Lineage Priest"**

As the Mother, you have the "Right of Entry" into the records of your child's life. You act as a **Judicial Intercessor** who stands between the "Past" of the ancestors and the "Future" of the seed.

**The Double Sided Defense:** You must intentionally name the giants of both sides. If the maternal side has a "spirit of fear" and the paternal side has a "spirit of lack," you legislate against both simultaneously. You are creating a **"New Bloodline Standard"** where the only thing that "travels" is the favor of God.

**1 Peter 1:18-19**

"Knowing that you were not redeemed with corruptible things, like silver or gold, from your aimless conduct received by tradition from your fathers, but with the precious blood of Christ, as of a lamb without blemish and without spot."

**The Judicial Link:** This is the **"Statute of Redemption."**

**The "Aimless Conduct" (The Tradition):** The Bible acknowledges that we receive "traditions" and "conduct" from our fathers (the bloodline). This includes the "Normalized Evil" and "Corrupted Data" we discussed.

**The Redemption Clause:** The word "redeemed" means to be released by the payment of a ransom.

**The Verdict:** This scripture gives you the legal right to say: *"My child has been* ***Ransomed*** *from the paternal and maternal traditions. The Blood of Christ which is without blemish is now the only 'Data' allowed to govern this child's life. I replace the 'Corruptible' heritage with the 'Precious' heritage!"*

**The Watchman's Sanitation Decree**

"I strike the Gavel and summon the 'Court of the Bloodline'! I present 1 Peter 1:18-19 as my Legal Evidence. I decree that my seed is officially **Redeemed** from the 'aimless conduct' and 'corrupted foundations' of both the maternal and paternal lineages!

I apply the 'Blood Solvent' to every ancestral lien. I scrub the spiritual DNA of my children! I command the spirit of addiction from maternal side and the spirit of premature death from paternal trait to **Disconnect** from this generation! I declare that the 'data' of the curse is **Deleted**, and the 'data' of the Covenant is **Uploaded**. I authorize a pure transfer of Kingdom virtues, and I veto every ancestral vice. My children shall not repeat the errors of their fathers, nor shall they carry the burdens of their mothers. A New Lineage begins today! In Jesus' Name!"

# Chapter 9: The Spiritual Map

***Gaining Discernment to See the Traps in your destiny, throne, star, Academics, Health, and Social Circles***

In the natural, you use a map to navigate unfamiliar terrain; in the spirit, **Discernment** is your GPS. As a Watchman, you are not just praying blindly; you are praying with **"Spirit Intelligence."** This chapter reveals that the enemy does not attack randomly; he sets "Strategic Traps" (snares) specifically tailored to your child's environment. To protect them, you must move beyond general prayers and begin to use the "Spiritual Map" to identify and dismantle these traps before your child steps into them.

### 1. Mapping the Academic Trap: The War for the Mind

The school system is not just a place of learning; it is a "Thought Atmosphere."

**The Snare of Ideology:** The enemy uses academics to plant seeds of "Intellectual Pride," "Atheistic Logic," or "Identity Confusion."

**The Intelligence Briefing:** Through discernment, you can "scan" the curriculum and the teachers. You can sense when a specific philosophy is being used as a "Trojan Horse" to enter your child's subconscious. You legislate to **"Jam the Signal"** of ungodly instruction so it cannot take root in their logic.

To explain the **Mapping of the Academic Trap**, we must recognize that the mind is the primary "Real Estate" the enemy seeks to occupy. In the spirit, an education is never neutral; it is an **Impartation**. When a child sits in a classroom, they are not just receiving data; they are breathing in an atmosphere that can either nourish their "Star" or suffocate their "Spirit."

### The Snare of Ideology: The "Counterfeit Truth"

The enemy uses the academic environment to build **"Strongholds of Logic."**

**Intellectual Pride:** This is the seed that teaches the child that their own intellect is the highest authority, effectively dethroning God as the Source of Wisdom.

**Atheistic Logic & Identity Confusion:** These are "Software Viruses" designed to crash the child's "Original Operating System" (their God given identity). By presenting these as "fact" or "progress," the enemy attempts to bypass the child's spiritual filters and embed "Normalized Confusion" into their character.

### The Intelligence Briefing: The "Spiritual X-Ray"

The "Intelligence Briefing" is your ability as a Watchman to perform a **"Spiritual Audit"** on the curriculum, the textbooks, and even the "Spirit" of the instructors.

**Detecting the Trojan Horse:** A philosophy may look like "Critical Thinking" or "Social Science," but discernment reveals the hidden spirit of rebellion or godlessness hidden inside. You are looking for the **"Subtext"** the message *behind* the message.

**Jamming the Signal:** In electronic warfare, jamming involves sending out a stronger frequency to block an enemy's communication. When you legislate, you are sending a **"Kingdom Frequency"** into your child's mind. You are decreeing that ungodly instruction will be "filtered out" and only the Truth will be "retained."

### Legislating the "Gate of the Ear and Eye"

As a Governor, you have the right to place a **"Spiritual Firewall"** over your child's ears and eyes while they are in school. You are decreeing that their subconscious is "Off Limits" to any data that contradicts the Word of God.

**2 Corinthians 10:4-5**

"For the weapons of our warfare are not carnal but mighty in God for pulling down strongholds, casting down arguments and every high thing that exalts itself against the knowledge of God, bringing every thought into captivity to the obedience of Christ."

**The Judicial Link:** This is the **"Master Warrant for Intellectual Defense."**

**Casting Down Arguments:** The "arguments" are the "logics" and "ideologies" taught in the classroom. This scripture gives you the legal authority to **"Pull Down"** an ungodly philosophy before it becomes a stronghold in your child's mind.

**Bringing Thought into Captivity:** This is a **"Search and Arrest"** order. You are authorized to "arrest" any thought or "academic seed" that tries to exalt itself above God's Truth. You are telling the school system: *"You may teach the curriculum, but you are forbidden from establishing a stronghold!"*

**The Watchman's Academic Interception Decree**

"I strike the Gavel and activate the 'Spiritual Firewall' over my child's mind! I invoke 2 Corinthians 10:4-5 and I decree that every ungodly argument, every atheistic logic, and every seed of identity confusion is **Pulled Down and Dismantled** before it can take root!

I 'Jam the Signal' of ungodly instruction! I decree that my child's ears and eyes are 'Sanctified Filters.' I forbid any 'Trojan Horse' of demonic philosophy from entering their subconscious. I command their 'Academic Intelligence' to be aligned with 'Kingdom Wisdom.' I bring every thought they receive in the classroom into captivity to the obedience of Christ. They shall have the Mind of Christ, and their logic shall be a weapon for the Kingdom, not a stronghold for the enemy! In Jesus' Name!"

### Mapping the Social Trap: The "Strange Fire" of Peer Influence

Social circles are the "Conduits of Culture." The enemy often uses a "Destiny Distractor" a friend or a romantic interest to lure a child off their "Star Path."

**Discerning the Spirit of the Circle:** Not every "nice" friend is a "safe" friend. Discernment allows you to see the **Spirit** behind the person. You can sense when a social circle carries a "Frequency of Rebellion" or "Stagnation."

**The Divine Reroute:** With your spiritual map, you see the "collision course" months before it happens. You legislate for the **"Severe Mercy"** of God to disconnect ungodly ties and attract "Destiny Helpers" who carry the scent of the Kingdom.

To explain **Mapping the Social Trap**, we must understand that relationships are **Transfers of Momentum**. In the spirit, no one is "just a friend." Every person in your child's social circle is a conduit for a specific spirit, and they are either accelerating your child toward their "Star Path" or "Distracting" them into a detour of delay.

### Discerning the Spirit of the Circle: The "Niceness" Mask

The enemy's most effective "Destiny Distractor" is rarely a "bad person" in the natural sense; they are often a "nice person" carrying a **Strange Fire**.

**The Frequency of Rebellion & Stagnation:** A social circle has a collective "climate." You may see a group of "good kids" who are "nice," but your spiritual map detects a frequency of **Stagnation** a spirit that makes your child lose their hunger for God, their passion for their books, or their respect for authority.

**The Mask of Influence:** Discernment allows you to see past the "nice" exterior to the **Spirit of the Influence**. You are looking at the "invisible leash." If a friend is "nice" but carries a spirit of

"Identity Confusion" or "Hidden Lust," that spirit will eventually try to leap onto your child through the conduit of their friendship.

**The "Divine Reroute: The Law of Severe Mercy**

Once you see a "Collision Course" on your spiritual map, you do not wait for the "wreck" to happen. You move into **Judicial Intervention**.

**The Legislative Disconnect:** You begin to pray for "Severe Mercy" a term for God's intervention that might be uncomfortable but is life saving. You ask God to "foul the air" between your child and a Destiny Distractor. You are legislating for a **Sovereign Friction** that makes the ungodly relationship impossible to maintain.

**Attracting Destiny Helpers:** While you are disconnecting the "Strange Fire," you are simultaneously "broadcasting" for **Destiny Helpers**. These are individuals who carry the "Scent of the Kingdom" people whose very presence activates the virtues in your child.

**The Law of the Conduit**

Social circles are the "nervous system" of a child's social development. If the conduit is corrupted, the "data" of their destiny cannot flow. By guarding the circle, you are ensuring that the only "data" entering your child's life is that which supports their "Throne Room" mandate.

**Proverbs 13:20**

"He who walks with wise men will be wise, but the companion of fools will be destroyed."

**The Judicial Link:** This is the **"Law of Spiritual Osmosis."**

**The Walking Clause:** The word "walks" implies a lifestyle and a shared journey. It proves that wisdom or folly is "caught" through proximity.

**The Companion of Fools:** The word for "companion" also means "to feed with" or "to be a friend of."

**The Verdict:** This scripture provides the legal basis for your "Reroute." You are telling the Court: *"I refuse to allow my child to be a 'Companion of Fools' because I refuse to allow them to be destroyed! Based on Proverbs 13:20, I demand a 'Divine Disconnect' from every foolish influence and a 'Supernatural Attachment' to the Wise!"*

**The Watchman's Social Disconnect Decree**

"I strike the Gavel and execute a 'Social Audit' over my child's circle! I invoke Proverbs 13:20 and declare that my seed shall walk **Only** with the wise! I 'Map Out' every Destiny Distractor and every Strange Fire masquerading as a friend!

I decree a 'Severe Mercy' over every ungodly tie! I command a 'Holy Friction' to arise between my child and any person seeking to lure them off their Star Path! I 'scramble the frequency' of ungodly influence and I snap the conduits of rebellion!

I broadcast for the 'Destiny Helpers'! I command the 'Wise Men and Women' of the Kingdom to appear in my child's path. I decree that my child is a magnet for those who carry the scent of the Throne! No longer shall my seed be a 'Companion of Fools'; they are now 'Walkers with the Wise.' The reroute is active! The circle is sanctified! In Jesus' Name!"

**Mapping the Health Trap: Identifying Symptomatic Warfare**

The enemy often hides in the physical body to mask a spiritual attack.

**The Root vs. The Symptom:** What looks like a "chronic allergy" or "sudden fatigue" may actually be a "Marine Monitoring Spirit" or an "Ancestral infirmity" trying to establish a foothold.

**The Diagnostic Scan:** As a mother, you have a "Prophetic Intuition." When you look at your child's health through the Spiritual Map, you aren't just looking at the body; you are looking at the **Life Force**. You can identify if an illness is a biological fluke or a "Legal Injunction" from the enemy trying to stop the child's momentum.

To explain **Mapping the Health Trap**, we must understand that the body is the "Physical Ground" where a spirit's destiny is anchored. If the enemy cannot stop the spirit, he will attempt to **sabotage the vessel**. In the spirit, "Symptomatic Warfare" is the use of physical ailments as "Legal Injunctions" to stall a child's momentum, drain the parents' resources, and distract the household from its spiritual mandate.

### The Root vs. The Symptom: Detecting the Injunction

A "biological fluke" is a natural occurrence that responds quickly to natural remedies. However, a **Spiritual Injunction** is an ailment that behaves like a "Legal Blockade."

**Marine Monitoring Spirits:** These often manifest as "fluid based" or "cycle based" issues (e.g., chronic respiratory congestion, recurring dreams of water followed by illness, or unexplained fatigue that hits exactly when a child is supposed to excel).

**Ancestral Infirmity:** This is a "Bloodline Malware." It is the enemy attempting to "install" a family weakness (like "the family heart condition" or "the family struggle with nerves") into the child's body to prove that they are still under the old lineage's laws.

**The Goal of the Trap:** The enemy isn't just attacking the body; he is trying to create a **"Pattern of Limitation."** If he can make a child believe they are "the sickly one," he has successfully caged a "Lion" before it can roar.

### The Diagnostic Scan: Prophetic Intuition

As a mother, you carry a **"Spiritual Stethoscope."** You have a biological and spiritual connection to your seed that allows you to perform a "Diagnostic Scan."

**canning the Life Force:** You aren't just looking at the thermometer; you are looking at the **Light** in their eyes and the **Peace** in their spirit.

**Identifying the "Legal" Source:** Through the Spiritual Map, you can sense if an illness has a "Voice." Does the sickness "speak" of fear? Does it arrive every time the child makes a spiritual leap? This is how you identify if you need a doctor, a prayer of deliverance, or a **Judicial Decree of Eviction.**

**Dismantling the Health Trap**

Once the trap is identified, you don't just "manage" the symptoms; you **revoke the legal right** of the infirmity to exist. You are legislating for "Divine Health," which is the state where the body is too "electrified" by the Spirit to host a demonic seed.

**Luke 13:11-12**

"And behold, there was a woman who had a spirit of infirmity eighteen years, and was bent over and could in no way raise herself up. But when Jesus saw her, He called her to Him and said to her, 'Woman, you are loosed from your infirmity.'

**The Judicial Link:** This is the **"Precedent for Symptomatic Warfare."**

**The Spirit of Infirmity:** Jesus did not diagnose this as a "calcium deficiency" or a "spinal misalignment." He identified the **Root** as a "Spirit." The symptom was physical (being bent over), but the source was a spiritual entity.

**The "Loosed" Decree:** The word "loosed" is a legal term meaning to set free, to discharge from a debt, or to **release from a legal bond.** **The Verdict:** This scripture proves that some health issues are actually "Illegal Bonds." You have the authority to say: *"I identify this recurring symptom as a 'Spirit of Infirmity.' Based on the precedent of Luke 13, I decree that my child is* ***Loosed****! I discharge the body from this demonic debt, and I command the spine, the blood, and the cells to stand upright!"*

**The Watchman's Health Diagnostic Decree**

"I strike the Gavel and activate my 'Prophetic Intuition' over my child's body! I refuse to be deceived by 'Symptomatic Warfare.' I invoke Luke 13:12 and I perform a 'Diagnostic Scan' on every recurring ailment and every spirit of fatigue!

I decree that my child is not a host for 'Ancestral Infirmity'! I identify any 'Marine Monitoring Spirit' trying to stall their momentum and I serve you an immediate 'Eviction Notice'! I declare that my child's body is the Temple of the Holy Ghost it is **Toxic** to the seeds of sickness and the germs of the enemy!

I command every 'Legal Injunction' against their health to be **Overturned**. I apply the Blood of Jesus to their DNA and I decree a 'Quiet Title' over their physical frame. You are **Loosed** from the bond of the infirmity! Rise up and walk in the fullness of your strength! In Jesus' Name!"

**Psalms 119:105**

"Your word is a lamp to my feet and a light to my path."

**The Judicial Link:** This is the **"Activated Map"** of the Believer.

**The Lamp to the Feet:** This is Immediate Discernment seeing the trap that is right in front of the child (a party, a specific conversation, a sudden mood shift).

**The Light to the Path:** This is Strategic Discernment seeing the long term trajectory of the child's life.

**The Verdict:** When you apply the Word as a "Light," you are asking the Holy Spirit to **X-ray** the environments your child enters. You are decreeing: *"Nothing is hidden that shall not be revealed! I command the Light of the Word to expose every hidden snare in the classroom, the locker room, and the social media feed!"*

**The Watchman's Map Decree**

"I strike the Gavel and activate the 'Eyes of the Spirit' over my household! I refuse to walk in blindness. I invoke Psalm 119:105 and decree that the Word of God is a 'Searchlight' over my child's academics, throne, destiny, wealthy, creativity, star, spiritual walk with God, circle of influence, health, and social circles!

I 'Map Out' the traps of the enemy and I dismantle them **Now!** I decree that every ungodly ideology in their school is neutralized by the Truth. I forbid any 'Destiny Distractor' from entering their social circle; I command a 'Divine Disconnect' from every person carrying a strange fire!

I scan their physical body with the Light of God, and I evict every hidden infirmity and symptomatic trap. I decree that my child's path is **'Lit Up'** by the Holy Ghost they shall not stumble, they shall not stray, and they shall not be snared! I see the trap, I name the trap, and I break the trap! In Jesus' Name!"

## Chapter 10: Breaking Lineage Traps

### *Disconnecting Your Sons and Daughters from Ancestral Cycles*

In the spirit realm, an **Ancestral Cycle** is a "Circulatory System of Failure." It is a demonic loop designed to ensure that every generation hits the same invisible ceiling. These traps are often "Time Activated" they lie dormant until a child reaches a certain age, a certain level of success, or a certain milestone (like marriage, career breakthrough, global visibility or childbearing), and then they "spring" to life to repeat the history of the fathers.

This chapter is your **"Deliverance Lab."** You are not just observing these patterns; you are performing the "Surgery of Disconnection." You are legally severing the "Spiritual Umbilical Cord" that ties your children to the errors, cycles, patterns, addictions, and limitations of their bloodline.

#### Identifying the "Time Activated" Trap

Ancestral traps are masterfully timed.

**The Cycle of Mid Life Collapse:** You may notice that in your lineage, everyone succeeds until age 30, then experiences a "crash" financial, moral, or physical.

**The Cycle of "Almost But Never":** This is the spirit of the "near success." It allows the child to get to the "Gate of Greatness" but never through it, because the same "Gatekeeper" that stopped the grandfather is now standing in the way of the grandson.

**The Lab Work:** As the Watchman, you must look at the "Calendar of the Lineage." When you see a recurring date or age of disaster, you are identifying a **Legal Landmark**. You legislate to "Cancel the Appointment" with that specific cycle.

To explain **Identifying the "Time Activated" Trap**, we must recognize that the enemy uses a "Spiritual Calendar." These are not random occurrences; they are **Scheduled Attacks** encoded into the bloodline. In the spirit, these traps act like "Landmines" buried in the soil of time, waiting for the child to reach a specific coordinate of age or achievement before they detonate.

### The Cycle of Mid Life Collapse: The "Age 30" Syndrome

The enemy often mimics divine timing with demonic counterfeits. Just as Jesus began His ministry at 30, the enemy may have a "reverse commissioning" scheduled for your lineage.

**The Invisible Ceiling:** You may see a pattern where the "Heirs" in your family are brilliant and rising until a specific age, then a "Sudden Storm" (divorce, bankruptcy, or health crisis) occurs.

**The Legal Landmark:** This isn't bad luck; it's a **Lineage Statute**. The enemy is enforcing a "Maturity Clause" that says: *"No one in this family is permitted to carry weight/power beyond this age."*

### The Cycle of "Almost But Never": The Gatekeeper's Toll

This is the trap of the **"Near Success."** It is designed to produce maximum frustration by allowing the child to see the "Promised Land" but never enter it.

**The Grandfather's Ghost:** If your grandfather was a great businessman who lost it all at the finish line, that same "Gatekeeper" (spirit of sabotaged success) is waiting for your son at that same "Gate."

**The Cycle of 99%:** The child gets 99% of the way to the breakthrough, the scholarship is almost signed, the contract is almost closed, and then a "freak accident" or a sudden change of heart by the decision makers stops it. This is a **Time Activated Blockade.**

### The Lab Work: Canceling the Appointment

As a Watchman, you must perform a **"Lineage Audit."** You look for the "Recurring Dates" the month your mother always got depressed, the age the men in the family always lost their jobs.

**Identifying the Landmark:** Once you find the date or age, you have found the **Legal Landmark** where the enemy has a "Reserved Seat" in your child's future.
**The Legislative Cancellation:** You don't wait for the age to arrive. You go into the "Lab of Prayer" now and **"Cancel the Appointment."** You are telling the Court: *"I identify the 30-year cycle of collapse. I move for a 'Motion to Vacate' this demonic appointment! This seat is already taken by the Holy Spirit!"*

**Habakkuk 2:3**

"For the vision is yet for an appointed time; but at the end it will speak, and it will not lie. Though it tarries, wait for it; because it will surely come, it will not tarry."

**The Judicial Link:** This is the **"Law of Appointed Times."**
**The Two Appointments:** In the spirit, there are "Appointed Times" for the Vision (God's plan) and "Appointed Times" for the Trap (the enemy's plan).
**The "Speaking" End:** The scripture says the "end will speak." When a time activated trap "speaks," it speaks of the failures of the past.
**The Verdict:** This scripture gives you the legal basis to prioritize **God's Appointment** over the **Enemy's Trap**. You are decreeing: *"I recognize the enemy's 'appointed time' for disaster, but I supersede it with God's 'appointed time' for the vision! I command the 'End' of my child's seasons to speak of Victory, not Collapse! The only thing that will 'surely come' is the fulfillment of the Word!"*

**The Watchman's Calendar Decree**

"I strike the Gavel and take my position over the 'Calendar of my Seed'! I refuse to allow the 'Scheduled Disasters' of my lineage to repeat in this generation! I invoke Habakkuk 2:3 and I declare that **Only** the God given vision has an appointed time in my children's lives!

I identify the 'Cycle of Mid Life Collapse' and the spirit of 'Almost But Never.' I serve an immediate 'Cancellation Notice' to every demonic appointment! I decree that the 'Gatekeepers' that stopped my ancestors are **Dismissed** and **Overruled**. My children shall pass through the Gates of Greatness with their 'Stars' intact!

I 'Scrub' the years 20, 30, 40, and 50 of my child's future. I remove every buried 'Landmine' of ancestral failure. I decree that their 'End' shall speak of the Glory of God! They shall not tarry in the wilderness of 'Almost'; they shall arrive 'On Time' in the Land of 'More Than Enough'! The trap is canceled; the Vision is established! In Jesus' Name!"

### The Mechanics of Spiritual Disconnection

Disconnection is a judicial act that revokes the "Law of Continuity."

**Severing the Cord:** Just as a doctor cuts the physical cord so the baby can breathe on its own, you must cut the spiritual cord that feeds your child the "Nutrients of the Curse."

**The "Stop Work" Order:** You are issuing a decree that the "Works of the Fathers" are no longer authorized to manifest in the lives of the "Heirs." You are declaring a **"Sovereign Discontinuity."**

To explain the **Mechanics of Spiritual Disconnection**, we must understand that in the spirit, a curse functions like a **Legacy Utility Line**. It is a spiritual pipe that was laid by previous generations, through which the "effluent" of ancestral iniquity continues to flow into the present. Disconnection is the judicial act of shutting off the valve and digging up the pipe so that the "Law of Continuity" is broken forever.

**Severing the Cord: Ending the "Curse Feed"**

In the natural, the umbilical cord is the lifeline; in the spirit, a "Lineage Cord" can become a "Death line."

**The Nutrients of the Curse:** If the ancestors lived on the "nutrients" of bitterness, addiction, occultism, witchcraft, freemason, sorcery, wizard, warlock or poverty, that cord is still trying to pump those same substances into your child's spirit. This is why a child might suddenly manifest a "taste" for the very sins that destroyed their grandfather.

**The Judicial Cut:** When you "Sever the Cord," you are performing a **Spiritual Omphalotomy**. You are decreeing that your child is no longer "plugged into" the old supply line. You are declaring: *"This child is now fed exclusively by the Root of Jesse and the River of Life. The feed of the lineage is CUT!"*

**The "Stop Work" Order: Sovereign Discontinuity**

In construction, a **Stop Work Order** is a legal notice that halts all activity on a site due to a violation of the law.

**The Works of the Fathers:** The enemy views your child's life as a "construction site" where he can finish the "Work of Destruction" he started in your parents. He wants to finish the "Tower of Pride" or the "Pit of Despair" that the previous generation began.

**Sovereign Discontinuity:** This is your decree that the "project" of the enemy has reached a dead end. You are declaring: *"There is no continuity here. The history of the fathers is a* ***Closed File****. The life of the heir is a* ***New Foundation.****"* You are forcing the enemy to pack up his "tools" and leave the site.

**Ephesians 2:14-15**

"For He Himself is our peace, who has made both one, and has broken down the middle wall of separation, having abolished in His flesh the enmity, that is, the law of commandments contained in ordinances, so as to create in Himself one new man from the two, thus making peace."

**The Judicial Link:** This is the **"Statute of the New Foundation."**
**Abolishing the Ordinances:** The "ordinances" are the **Lineage Laws** the spiritual "handwriting" that says "this family must suffer."
**Breaking the Middle Wall:** This is the ultimate act of **Disconnection**. Christ broke the "wall" that allowed the "enmity" (the curse) to travel.
**The "One New Man":** This is the legal basis for **Sovereign Discontinuity**. You are telling the Court: *"My child is not a 'continuation' of the old man; they are a 'New Man' in Christ. The old 'ordinances' of my bloodline have been* ***Abolished****. There is no longer a legal conduit for the enmity of the past to reach the peace of the present!"*

**The Watchman's Disconnection Decree**

"I strike the Gavel and execute the 'Mechanics of Disconnection' over my seed! I invoke Ephesians 2:15 and declare that the 'Law of Ordinances' the spiritual rules of my bloodline are officially ABOLISHED!

I 'Sever the Cord' that has pumped the nutrients of the curse into this generation. I command the spiritual umbilical cord to the past to wither and die! I issue a 'Stop Work Order' against every ancestral spirit trying to build a 'Tower of Failure' in my child's life. I declare a 'Sovereign Discontinuity'!

I decree that my children are 'New Men and New Women' in Christ. They are not a 'sequel' to their ancestors' stories; they are a 'New Creation' with a New Beginning. I disconnect the pipe, I break the wall, and I seal the breach! The flow of the past stops Here! In Jesus' Name!"

**Liberating the Heirs: From "Inheritance of Debt" to "Inheritance of Light"**

In a corrupted lineage, children inherit "Spiritual Debt." Liberation means the "Debt" is settled by the Blood, and the "Account" is closed.

**The New Foundation:** You are moving your children from the "Quicksand" of ancestral patterns onto the "Rock" of the Finished Work. You are decreeing that they are now **"First Generation Heirs of the New Covenant,"** with no link to the old ledger.

To explain **Liberating the Heirs**, we must view the transition as a **Transference of Titles**. In a corrupted lineage, a child is born into a "Negative Estate" an inheritance defined by spiritual bankruptcy and the "debt" of iniquity. Liberation is the judicial process of closing that insolvent account and opening a **Kingdom Trust** that is pre funded by the Finished Work of Christ.

**Closing the "Account of Debt"**

In the spirit, "Spiritual Debt" is the accumulated legal claim the enemy has over a bloodline due to unpaid "moral taxes" (sins, inequity, covenants, and rebellions).

**The Negative Balance:** When a child inherits debt, they start life in the "red." They have to work twice as hard for half the results because the "interest" on ancestral sin is constantly draining their spiritual and physical resources.

**The Settlement:** Liberation is not a "negotiation" with the enemy; it is a **Settlement by the Blood**. You are presenting the Court of Heaven with a payment that is greater than the debt. You are decreeing: *"The account of the Family Name lineage is* ***Closed****. The debt is zeroed out by the Precious Blood of the Lamb. No collector has a right to call on this seed!"*

**The New Foundation: From Quicksand to Rock**

Ancestral patterns are like **Quicksand**, the more the child tries to struggle out of the "family temper" or "family poverty," the deeper they sink, because the foundation itself is unstable.

**First Generation Heirs:** You are legislating for a **"Foundation Swap."** You are lifting your children off the sinking sand of their natural heritage and placing them on the **Rock of the New Covenant**.

**No Link to the Old Ledger:** This means their "Credit Score" in the spirit is no longer tied to their grandfather's failures. They are now "First Generation Heirs," meaning they start with a clean record, a full inheritance, and the "First Born Rights" of Christ Himself.

**Colossians 1:12-13**

"Giving thanks to the Father who has qualified us to be partakers of the inheritance of the saints in the light. He has delivered us from the power of darkness and conveyed us into the kingdom of the Son of His love."

**The Judicial Link:** This is the **"Deed of Conveyance."**

**The Qualification:** You don't "earn" the liberation of your heirs; the Father "qualifies" them. You are legislating based on **Divine Eligibility**, not human merit.

**The Conveyance:** In law, **Conveyance** is the legal transfer of property from one entity to another. This scripture proves that your children have been **Legally Transferred**.

**The Verdict:** You are telling the Court: *"My children have been 'Conveyed.' They no longer belong to the 'Jurisdiction of Darkness' (the debt filled lineage). They have been moved to the 'Jurisdiction of Light.' All old liens are stayed! All old debts are void! The title has been transferred to the Kingdom of the Son!"*

**The Watchman's Conveyance Decree**

"I strike the Gavel and authorize a 'Supernatural Transference' over my seed! I invoke Colossians 1:13 and declare that my children are officially **Conveyed** out of the power of darkness and the 'Inheritance of Debt'!

I close the old 'Family Ledger' and I seal it with the Blood of Jesus! I decree that my children are 'First Generation Heirs of the New Covenant.' They are no longer liable for the spiritual bankruptcy of their ancestors. I move them from the 'Quicksand' of the past onto the 'Rock' of the Finished Work!

I decree that they are 'Qualified Partakers' of the Inheritance of Light. Every 'Debt Collector' spirit is hereby served a 'Permanent Injunction.' You cannot touch their health, you cannot touch their wealth, and you cannot touch their peace. The account is settled! The Title is transferred! The Heirs are FREE! In Jesus' Name!"

**The Anchor Scripture: Ezekiel 18:2-3**

"What do you mean by repeating this proverb concerning the land of Israel, 'The fathers have eaten sour grapes, and the children's teeth are set on edge'? 'As I live,' says the Lord God, 'you shall no longer have occasion to use this proverb in Israel.'"

**The Judicial Link:** This is the **"Statute of Individual Liberty."**

**The Sour Grapes Proverb:** This is the biblical description of an **Ancestral Cycle**. It describes a "Biological Reaction" in the children based on an "Action" taken by the fathers. It's the idea that "because my father did it, I must suffer for it."

**The "No Longer" Injunction:** God Himself issues a **Restraining Order** against the proverb. He is declaring that the cycle of "Trans generational Consequence" is officially **Decommissioned** for His people.

**The Verdict:** This scripture gives you the legal right to stand before the Court and say: *"I strike this 'Proverb' from my child's life! I refuse the* *'teeth on edge' syndrome! According to Ezekiel 18, the occasion for this cycle to repeat has* ***Been Terminated*** *by Divine Decree!"*

### The Watchman's Disconnection Decree

"I strike the Gavel and enter the 'Deliverance Lab' over my seed! I present Ezekiel 18:3 as my Supreme Court Evidence! I decree that the 'Proverb' of my lineage is **Broken!** My fathers may have eaten 'sour grapes,' but I declare that my children's teeth **Shall Not** be set on edge!

I 'Sever the Cord' of ancestral continuity! I disconnect my sons and daughters from the cycle of [name the cycle: e.g., divorce, poverty, addiction, delay]. I command every 'Time Activated Trap' to be dismantled **Now**! You shall not crash at the age your father crashed; you shall not fail where your mother failed!

I declare a 'Sovereign Discontinuity' between the past of this bloodline and the future of this generation! I close the 'Ancestral Account' and I open the 'Kingdom Ledger.' My children are First Generation Heirs of Glory! The cycle ends with me; the Crown begins with them! In Jesus' Name!"

# Chapter 11: The "Touch Not" Generation

## *Encasing Your Family in the Wall of Fire and the Blood of the Lamb*

In the hierarchy of spiritual security, there is a level of protection known as **"Sovereign Immunity."** This is the stage where your family moves from "fighting for victory" to "dwelling in the secret place." This chapter deals with the creation of a **Dual Layered Defense System**: the internal cleansing of the **Blood** and the external perimeter of the **Fire**.

When a family is encased in this way, they become a **"Touch Not" Generation**. This is not a suggestion to the enemy; it is a spiritual law that triggers immediate consequences for any entity that attempts to breach the boundary.

### 1. The Internal Seal: The Blood of the Lamb

The Blood of Jesus is the **"Spiritual DNA Marker"** that identifies your family as Kingdom Property.

**The "Passover" Protocol:** Just as the blood on the doorposts in Egypt signaled to the Destroyer that the house was "Off Limits," the Blood of the Lamb creates a "Legal Cloak" over your children. It renders them "unswallowable" to the enemy.

**The Cleansing Stream:** The Blood doesn't just protect; it constantly "sanitizes" the atmosphere of the home, ensuring that no "Internal Breach" (sin or discord) can stay long enough to attract an "External Attack."

To explain the **Internal Seal of the Blood**, we must understand that in the spirit realm, the Blood of Jesus acts as a **Frequency of Ownership**. It is a "living substance" that speaks in the Courtroom of Heaven, establishing a "Legal Cloak" that prevents the enemy from even identifying your children as potential targets.

**The "Passover" Protocol: The Legal Cloak**

In the original Exodus account, the blood was not for the people inside to see; it was for the **Destroyer** to see.

**The "Off Limits" Signal:** When you apply the Blood to your children, you are applying a **"Spiritual Barcode"** that reads: *Property of the Kingdom of God; Jurisdiction of the Most High.*

**Un swallowable to the Enemy:** In the spirit, the enemy is described as a roaring lion seeking whom he may "devour." However, the Blood makes your child "distasteful" and "unswallowable" to the demonic. It acts as a **Legal Cloak,** an invisibility shield that hides their destiny from the "predatory gaze" of the kingdom of darkness.

**The Cleansing Stream: Atmospheric Sanitation**

The Blood of Jesus is not a static "paint"; it is a **Continuous Stream.**

**Closing the Internal Breach:** An "External Attack" often requires an "Internal Breach" (a legal landing strip of discord, unconfessed sin, or bitterness) to latch onto.

**The Self Cleaning Atmosphere:** By invoking the Blood, you are installing a **"Spiritual Air Purification System."** The Blood "speaks" better things than the blood of Abel (Hebrews 12:24). While Abel's blood cried for *vengeance*, Jesus' Blood cries for *mercy and cleansing.* It "sanitizes" the home by constantly washing away the "scent" of human error that might otherwise attract a demonic scavenger.

**Exodus 12:13**

"Now the blood shall be a sign for you on the houses where you are. And when I see the blood, I will pass over you; and the plague shall not be on you to destroy you when I strike the land of Egypt."

**The Judicial Link:** This is the **"Statute of the Protective Mark."**

**The "Sign"** In Hebrew, a "sign" is a signal, a monument, or a **distinguishing mark.** It is a piece of "Evidence" presented to the spiritual atmosphere.
**The "Pass Over"):** This does not just mean "to go by." It means to "hover over" or "protectively leap." When God saw the blood, He stood as a **Guard at the Door** to prevent the Destroyer from entering.
**The Verdict:** This scripture provides the legal precedent for **Exemption**. You are telling the Court: *"I present the Blood as the 'Sign' over my seed! According to Exodus 12:13, the plague of [depression, addiction, prostitution, spiritual dwarfism, poverty, sickness, rebellion] has NO LEGAL RIGHT to enter this house. The Destroyer is served a 'No Entry' order because the Blood is speaking at the Gate!"*

### The Watchman's Blood Seal Decree

"I strike the Gavel and apply the 'Internal Seal of the Blood' over the doorposts of my children's souls! I invoke Exodus 12:13 and declare that my family is officially EXEMPT from the plagues of this generation!

I activate the 'Passover Protocol'! I decree that my seed is 'un swallowable' to the enemy. I apply the Blood as a 'Legal Cloak' that hides their destiny from every monitoring spirit and every predatory entity. I 'Sanitize' the atmosphere of my home; let the Blood wash away every internal breach, every word of discord, and every landing strip for the enemy!

I decree that the Blood is 'Speaking' over my children! It speaks Peace, it speaks Protection, and it speaks Ownership. My house is a 'No Go Zone' for the Destroyer! When the enemy sees the Mark, he must 'Pass Over' and move on! In Jesus' Name!"

### The External Perimeter: The Wall of Fire

While the Blood seals the *content*, the Fire encases the *container*.

**The Invisible Fence:** The "Wall of Fire" is a high frequency spiritual barrier. To the natural eye, your house looks like any other; in the spirit, it is a **Pillar of Blazing Light**.
**The "Incineration" Clause:** Any curse, monitoring spirit, or "assigned arrow" that hits this wall is not just stopped it is **Incinerated**. This is the defense system of the "Zion-Class" home. It ensures that the enemy cannot even "park" in front of your gate to observe your seed.

To explain the **Wall of Fire**, we must move from the concept of a "gate" to the concept of a **"Sovereign Perimeter."** While the Blood deals with the *legal right* of the enemy to enter, the Fire deals with the *physical proximity* of the enemy to your seed. This is **Active Defense Technology** for the Zion Class home.

### The Invisible Fence: The Pillar of Blazing Light

In the natural, your home has walls of wood and stone; in the spirit, it is surrounded by a **High Frequency Barrier**.
**The Frequency of the Consuming Fire:** God is a "Consuming Fire" (Hebrews 12:29). When you legislate for the Wall of Fire, you are pulling the very nature of God's Presence out into the yard.
**The Blinding Light:** Monitoring spirits rely on "visual data" they watch your children's routines, moods, and weaknesses. The Wall of Fire acts as a **"Flash Blind"** to the kingdom of darkness. It turns your home into a "Sun" in the spirit realm; the enemy cannot look at it, much less study it. You are creating a **"Blackout Zone"** for demonic intelligence.

### The "Incineration" Clause: Total Destruction of Inbound Arrows

Most people pray for a "shield" to stop arrows, but a shield implies that the arrow still exists and can be picked up and reused. The **Incineration Clause** is different.
**Instant Combustion:** When an assigned arrow of infirmity, a curse of delay, or a spirit of "Strange Fire" hits the Wall of Fire, it doesn't

just bounce off; it is **atomized**. The Fire consumes the "DNA" of the attack.

**The "No Parking" Zone:** Monitoring spirits often "camp" or "park" at the gates of a destiny to wait for a moment of vulnerability. The Wall of Fire makes the "sidewalk" of your child's life too hot for the enemy to stand on. It forces the enemy into a permanent retreat because the very atmosphere of your property is **lethal** to their presence.

**The Zion Class Defense System**

A "Zion Class" home is one that has been legislated into the same security status as the New Jerusalem. It is a place where the "Glory" and the "Fire" meet. By encasing your container in Fire, you ensure that your children are raised in a **"Sterile Environment"** free from the atmospheric pollutants of the world's spirit.

**Psalms 97:3**

"A fire goes before Him, and burns up His enemies round about."

**The Judicial Link:** This is the **"Advance Guard Statute."**

**The "Before Him" Clause:** The Fire doesn't wait for the attack to reach the house; it goes *out* to meet it. This is **Preemptive Warfare**.

**The "Round About" Clause:** Just like in Zechariah, this is a 360-degree radius of destruction.

**The Verdict:** This scripture gives you the authority to set the "Rules of Engagement" for your property. You are telling the spirit world: *"I invoke Psalm 97:3! I release a 'Forward Operating' Fire around my seed. I decree that any entity that comes 'round about' my children with evil intent is automatically* ***Subject to Combustion****. The Fire is the Judge, and the verdict is 'Incineration'!"*

**The Watchman's Incineration Decree**

"I strike the Gavel and activate the 'Incineration Clause' over the perimeter of my family! I invoke Psalm 97:3 and declare that a Fire goes before my children and burns up their enemies round about!

I decree that my home is a 'Pillar of Blazing Light'! I 'Scramble the Vision' of every monitoring spirit. I command a 'Flash Blind' to hit every demonic eye trying to observe my seed! You cannot park at my gate, you cannot camp in my atmosphere, and you cannot track our movements!

I declare that every 'Assigned Arrow' of sickness, poverty, addiction, rebellion, or delay is **Incinerated** the moment it touches our Wall of Fire! I refuse to just 'block' the attack; I command the total atomization of the weapon! My family is encased in a Zion Class Defense System. The air we breathe is Holy, the ground we walk on is Fire, and the atmosphere we carry is Glory! In Jesus' Name!"

**Activating "Touch Not" Status**

To be a "Touch Not" generation means you have reached a **Judicial Standing** where the Court of Heaven has issued a "Permanent Protective Order" over your lineage.

**The Mark of Ownership:** You are decreeing that your children carry the "Marks of the Lord Jesus," which act as a **"No Fly Zone"** for demonic activity.

**The Atmosphere of Glory:** When a family is encased in Fire, they no longer breathe the "oxygen of the world"; they breathe the "atmosphere of the Glory," which makes them resilient to the diseases and depressions of the age.

To explain **Activating "Touch Not" Status**, we must understand that this is the highest level of **Executive Immunity** available to a family. It is a transition from asking for protection to **Enforcing a Permanent Injunction**. In the spirit, you are moved from the "General Population" of the world into a "Protected Class" under the direct sovereignty of the King.

### The Mark of Ownership: The "No Fly Zone"

In the natural, a "No-Fly Zone" is an area where unauthorized aircraft are subject to immediate interception and destruction. In the spirit, the **"Marks of the Lord Jesus"** (the *Stigmata* of ownership) serve as your child's "Aeronautical Credentials."

**The Judicial Mark:** These marks are not visible to the natural eye, but they are "Infrared Beacons" in the spirit. When a demonic entity attempts to "fly over" your child's mind, health, or social life, they encounter the **"Mark of Ownership."**

**Self-Executing Protection:** This status means the protection is "Automatic." You don't always have to be awake to pray; the Mark itself carries a "Voice" that tells every intruder: *"This property is already spoken for. Unauthorized entry will result in immediate judicial retaliation."*

### The Atmosphere of Glory: Spiritual Resilience

Most of the world breathes the "Oxygen of the Age" an atmosphere saturated with the "Data" of depression, anxiety, and viral fear. However, a "Touch Not" family breathes a different "Chemical Compound": **The Glory.**

**Atmospheric Resilience:** When your children breathe the "Atmosphere of the Glory," their spiritual and physical immune systems are upgraded. They become **Resilient to the Age**.

**The "Weight" of Zion:** The word *Kavod* (Glory) literally means "Weight." You are decreeing that your children carry a spiritual "Heaviness" that makes them "unshakable." While other children are being blown away by the "winds of culture," your "Touch Not" generation is anchored by the weight of the Presence.

### The Permanent Protective Order

Activating this status means you have presented the "Title Deeds" of your lineage to the Court of Heaven and received a **Final**

**Decree**. This is a "Restraining Order" that does not expire. It is handed to the principalities of your region, informing them that your seed is **"Non Negotiable Property."**

**Psalm 105:14-15**

"He permitted no man to do them wrong; Yes, He rebuked kings for their sakes, saying, 'Do not touch My anointed ones, and do My prophets no harm.'"

**The Judicial Link:** This is the **"Statute of Sovereign Immunity."**

**The "No Man" Clause:** This is a **Total Prohibition**. It doesn't say "He limited the wrong," it says He "permitted NO man."

**Rebuking Kings:** This proves that your "Touch Not" status overrules even the "High Ranking" spirits (Kings/Principalities) of your region.

**The Verdict:** You are telling the Court: *"I invoke the 'Touch Not' Statute of Psalm 105! I decree that my children are the 'Anointed Ones' of this generation. I demand a 'Permanent Protective Order' that rebukes every demonic king and every social architect that seeks to do them harm! The Gavel has fallen:* ***Touch Not!"***

**The Watchman's "Touch Not" Activation Decree**

"I strike the Gavel and activate the 'Touch Not' Status over my lineage! I invoke Psalm 105:15 and declare that my children are the 'Anointed Seed' of the Most High! I decree a 'No-Fly Zone' over their minds, stars, breakthroughs, academics, spiritual walk with God, their bodies, and their destinies!

I apply the 'Mark of Ownership' the Marks of the Lord Jesus to their spiritual foreheads! Every demonic entity, every monitoring spirit, and every social intruder is hereby served a 'Permanent Restraining Order.' You are **Forbidden** from touching this seed!

I decree that my family breathes the 'Atmosphere of the Glory'! We are resilient to the depressions and diseases of this age! We carry the 'Weight of Zion,' and we shall not be moved! I stand in my Judicial Standing and I declare the verdict of Heaven: My children are **Untouchable, Un Stoppable, And Un Shakable!** In Jesus' Name!"

**Zechariah 2:5**

"'For I,' says the Lord, 'will be a wall of fire all around her, and I will be the glory in her midst.'"

**The Judicial Link:** This is the **"Statute of Total Enclosure."**

**The "All Around" Clause:** Means a complete circle, a perimeter without a gap. This verse proves that God does not just protect your "front door"; He creates a **360-Degree Defense**.

**The "Glory in the Midst":** This is the internal component. The Fire keeps the enemy *out*, while the Glory keeps the family *pure*.

**The Verdict:** This scripture provides the legal "Security Blueprint" for your home. You are telling the Court: *"Based on Zechariah 2:5, I demand the activation of the Fire-Wall! I decree that the perimeter of my family is 'White Hot' and the center of my family is 'Glory Filled'! Any intruder attempting to cross the line must face the Consuming Fire of God!"*

**The Watchman's "Touch Not" Decree**

"I strike the Gavel and activate the 'Sovereign Immunity' of my household! I invoke Zechariah 2:5 and I decree that the Lord is a **Wall of Fire** all around my seed, and the **Glory** in our midst!

I apply the Blood of the Lamb to the 'Digital and Spiritual Doorposts' of my children's lives. I declare them 'Touch Not' property! I 'Scramble the Sensors' of every monitoring spirit; you cannot see them, you cannot track them, and you cannot touch them!

I decree that every arrow of infirmity, every bullet of rebellion, and every curse of delay is **Incinerated** the moment it touches the Wall of Fire around my home! We are encased in the Blood and surrounded by the Flame. My children are a 'No Fly Zone' for the kingdom of darkness! They shall walk in the midst of the Fire and not be burned, for they ARE the fire! In Jesus' Name!"

# Chapter 12: Virtue Recovery

## *Reclaiming Every Star, Gift, and Inheritance the Enemy Attempted to Exchange*

In the spiritual marketplace, the enemy is known as a **"Merchant of Souls."** His primary strategy is the **"Illegal Exchange"** swapping a child's "Star" (their bright, God given destiny) for a life of mediocrity, or trading their "Virtue" (their inherent spiritual power and character) for a "Counterfeit Identity."

**Virtue Recovery** is the judicial process of **Restitution**. It is the stage where the Watchman enters the enemy's "Warehouse of Stolen Goods" and demands the immediate return of everything that was siphoned, traded, or hidden from the child's lineage.

### The "Illegal Exchange" and the "Substitution" Trap

The enemy often uses "Life Altering Traps" to facilitate an exchange.

**The Siphoned Star:** This happens when a child's brilliance, creativity, or leadership "Star" is siphoned off to fuel another's agenda, or when it is buried under the "shame" of an ancestral sin.

**The Gift Swap:** This is the "Esau Syndrome," where a child is tempted to trade their "Birthright" (their spiritual giftings) for a "Bowl of Stew" (temporary pleasure, selling souls to satan or social acceptance).

**The Recovery Protocol:** You are legislating to **"Void the Transaction."** You are telling the spirit world: *"The exchange made by the ancestors is **Null**. The trade my child attempted to make in a moment of weakness is **Void**. I demand the return of the Original Virtue!"*

To explain the **"Illegal Exchange" and the "Substitution" Trap**, we must understand that the enemy is a **Counterfeit Merchant**. He knows he cannot create "Stars" or "Gifts," so he must steal them from the Kingdom's heirs. He uses "Life Altering Traps" to trick a child into a spiritual trade off, where they give up their eternal "Weight of Glory" for a temporary "Shadow of Satisfaction."

### The Siphoned Star: The "Vampiric" Trade

In the spirit, a "Star" is the **Visible Frequency** of a child's destiny (Matthew 2:2).

**The Siphoning Effect:** The enemy attempts to "tap into" a child's brilliance or leadership and redirect that energy to fuel ungodly systems or even other people's agendas. A child may be the "brain" behind a project, but someone else gets the credit and the reward.

**The Burial of Shame:** Alternatively, the enemy uses the "Shame of Ancestral Sin" to convince the child that their Star is "too dirty" to shine. He buries their creativity under the weight of a family "label" (e.g., "we are just laborers," or "we aren't the academic type").

### The Gift Swap: The "Esau Syndrome"

This is a **High Level Substitution Trap**.

**The Birthright vs. The Stew:** Esau had the "Birthright" (the legal right to the double portion and the lineage of the Messiah), but he traded it for "Stew" (instant gratification).

**The Trap of Acceptance:** For a child, the "Stew" is often **Social Validation**. The enemy says: *"Trade your spiritual sensitivity for 'coolness.' Trade your prophetic voice for 'fitting in.'"* Once the child agrees to the trade, the enemy attempts to finalize the contract in the spiritual court.

### The Recovery Protocol: Voiding the Transaction

As a Governor, you are the **Public Prosecutor** for your child's destiny.

**Legislation of Rescission:** In law, "Rescission" is the unmaking of a contract. You are declaring that any contract signed in a state of "Demonic Duress" or "Ancestral Ignorance" is **Legally Non-Binding**.

**Demanding the Original Virtue:** You aren't asking for a "replacement"; you are demanding the **Original, High Grade Virtue** that God placed in their spirit before the foundation of the world.

**Isaiah 49:24-25**

"Shall the prey be taken from the mighty, or the captives of a righteous warrior be delivered? But thus says the Lord: 'Even the captives of the mighty shall be taken away, and the prey of the terrible be delivered; for I will contend with him who contends with you, and I will save your children.'"

**The Judicial Link:** This is the **"Statute of Divine Repossession."**

**The "Lawful Captive" Argument:** The enemy often argues: *"I have a right to this Star because the child/ancestor traded it to me fairly."* (The "Righteous Warrior's Captive").

**The "But Thus Says the Lord" Override:** This is the **Supreme Court Injunction**. God declares that even if the trade seemed "legal" in the past, He is **Nullifying the Contract**.

**The Verdict:** You are telling the Court: *"I invoke Isaiah 49! The prey shall be delivered! I don't care how 'mighty' the entity is that holds my child's Star God is contending with them! I declare the 'Gift Swap' VOID and I demand the release of the 'Prey' (the stolen virtue) immediately!"*

**The Watchman's "Void and Recover" Decree**

"I strike the Gavel and enter a 'Motion to Void' every illegal exchange in my child's lineage! I invoke Isaiah 49:25 and I declare that the 'Prey of the Terrible' **Must Be Delivered!**

I identify every 'Siphoned Star' and I command the spiritual 'Siphons' to be broken NOW! I 'Void' the Esau Syndrome in my seed; I decree that my children shall NOT trade their Birthright for the 'Stew' of this world! I cancel every contract of social acceptance that required a sacrifice of spiritual virtue!

I 'Rescind' every trade made by my ancestors that gave away the 'Brilliance' of this bloodline! I demand the return of the Original Virtue! I decree that my child's Star is being dug out from the 'Soil of Shame' and is now being polished by the Spirit of God! The 'Mighty' must let go; the 'Terrible' must surrender! My children's gifts are **Coming Home!** In Jesus' Name!"

### Reclaiming the "Stolen Inheritance"

Inheritance is not just money; it is **Spiritual Momentum.**

**The "Lent" Virtue:** Many times, the "Stars" of a family are "on loan" to the kingdom of darkness because of unholy covenants.

**The Repossession Order:** As a mother, you are issuing a **"Writ of Repossession."** You are identifying every gift that "skipped a generation" or every talent that was "stolen" by addiction and you are commanding it to manifest in your child. You are decreeing: *"That which was stolen from the grandfather shall be recovered by the grandson!"*

To explain **Reclaiming the "Stolen Inheritance,"** we must shift our perspective from seeing inheritance as physical assets to seeing it as **Spiritual Equity**. In the Kingdom, an inheritance is the "Cumulative Favor" and "Prophetic Momentum" intended to build over generations. When this is stolen, the lineage feels "spiritually dry," and each generation has to start from zero because the "wealth of the spirit" has been diverted.

### The "Lent" Virtue: The Illegal Lease

In many bloodlines, the "Stars" the high level gifts of administration, wealth creation, or spiritual authority are currently **"On Loan"** to the kingdom of darkness.

**The Unholy Covenant:** This happens when an ancestor traded the "Gifts of the Seed" for protection, power, or temporary relief. The enemy essentially "leases" the family's virtue to power his own systems.

**The "Skip Generation" Syndrome:** You may notice a brilliant talent that appeared in a great grandfather, vanished in the father, and is trying to spark in the child. That gap is often a **Spiritual Embargo**. The enemy has placed a "Lien" on that gift, preventing it from manifesting until the "debt" is addressed.

### The Repossession Order: The "Writ of Assistance"

As a Governor and a Watchman, you are not just "asking" for the inheritance; you are issuing a **Writ of Repossession**.

**The Judicial Search:** You are looking back through the "Lineage Records" and identifying the "Missing Pieces." If your grandfather was a pioneer who never saw the fruit, or your mother was a singer whose voice was "stolen" by depression, you are identifying that **Specific Equity**.

**The Grandson's Recovery:** You are decreeing a **"Generational Catch Up."** You are telling the spirit world: *"The time for the 'Lease' has expired! I am here to repossess the momentum of the fathers for the use of the sons! Every gift that was hijacked by addiction or buried by trauma is hereby* ***Summoned*** *to manifest in my child!"*

### Spiritual Momentum: The "Compound Interest" of Glory

When you reclaim the inheritance, your child doesn't just start where you left off; they start with the **Accumulated Power** of the entire righteous lineage. You are legislating for a "Double Portion" that includes the unfulfilled promises of those who came before.

**Joel 2:25**

"So I will restore to you the years that the swarming locust has eaten, the crawling locust, the consuming locust, and the chewing locust, My great army which I sent among you."

**The Judicial Link:** This is the **"Statute of Total Restoration."**

**The Four Locusts:** These represent the various ways the inheritance was stolen some through sudden "swarming" crises, some through the slow "chewing" of daily addiction or delay.

**The "I Will Restore" Decree:** This is a **Sovereign Reversal**. God is not just replacing the "crop"; He is replacing the **"Years."** He is restoring the **Time and Momentum** that was lost.

**The Verdict:** You are telling the Court: *"I invoke the Joel 2:25 Restitution Clause! The locusts of my bloodline have eaten enough! I demand the restoration of the 'Years' of my ancestors! I decree that the momentum stolen from the previous generations is now being* ***Compressed*** *and* ***Released*** *into the life of my child! The years of theft are now years of acceleration!"*

### The Watchman's Repossession Decree

"I strike the Gavel and issue a 'Writ of Repossession' over my child's inheritance! I invoke Joel 2:25 and I decree that the 'Years' eaten by the locusts of my bloodline are being RESTORED to my seed **Now**!

I 'Terminate the Lease' on every lent virtue! I command every gift, every talent, and every 'Star' that was on loan to the kingdom of darkness to be returned to this generation! I identify the [name specific gift, e.g., the gift of wealth, the gift of music, the gift of leadership] and I command it to manifest in my child!

I decree that the 'Skip Generation' embargo is **Broken**! That which was stolen from the fathers is now the property of the children! I reclaim the spiritual momentum of my lineage! My child shall not start from zero; they shall start from the 'Peak' of the previous generation's victory! The locusts are defeated, the inheritance is returned, and the momentum is MINE! In Jesus' Name!"

### Activating the "Seven Fold Restitution"

In the Kingdom Court, the penalty for theft is not just a return; it is a **Multiplication**.

**The Interest of Heaven:** You aren't just getting back what was lost; you are reclaiming it with the "interest" of the years the locusts have eaten. This is where your child moves from "Recovery" into "Abundance."

**Proverbs 6:31**

"Yet when he is found, he must restore sevenfold; he may have to give up all the substance of his house."

**The Judicial Link:** This is the **"Mandatory Sentencing Guideline for Spiritual Theft."**

**The "When He is Found" Clause:** This is the moment of **Exposure**. By reading this chapter and identifying the stolen virtue, you have "found" the thief.

**The "Sevenfold" Requirement:** This is a **Judicial Penalty**. It means the enemy cannot just "stop" the attack; he must pay back seven times the "glory," seven times the "favor," and seven times the "momentum" he stole.

**The Verdict:** You are telling the Court: *"The thief has been found! I present the evidence of the 'stolen star' and the 'exchanged virtue.' According to Proverbs 6:31, I demand a* ***Sevenfold Restitution*** *over my seed! I command the enemy to empty his 'house' to restore the substance of my children!"*

**The Watchman's Recovery Decree**

"I strike the Gavel and enter the 'Warehouse of the Enemy'! I expose the 'Thief' and I declare that the 'Illegal Exchange' is **Void!** I invoke Proverbs 6:31 and I demand the **Immediate Restoration** of every star, every gift, and every inheritance that was stolen from my lineage!

I 'Void the Transaction' of the Esau Syndrome! I decree that my child's birthright is restored! Every 'Star' that was siphoned by ancestral altars is now **Reclaimed**. I command every stolen talent, every buried dream, and every hijacked opportunity to be returned to my seed **Now** with **Sevenfold Interest!**

I 'Repossess' the spiritual momentum of my fathers! I decree that the 'Substance' of the enemy's house must be released to fund the destiny of my heirs! What was lost in the past is recovered in the present! My children shall walk in a 'Surplus of Virtue' and a 'Double Portion' of Favor! The thief is caught, the Gavel has fallen, and the Recovery is **Complete**! In Jesus' Name!"

# Chapter 13: Securing The Virtues

## *Locking in Wealth, Creativity, and Longevity Before Adulthood*

In the spirit realm, there is a "Window of Vulnerability" that exists before a child reaches the legal and spiritual age of accountability. If the enemy cannot stop a child from being born with "Stars," he will wait for the transition into adulthood to "Tax," "Loot," or "Foreclose" on their virtues.

**Securing the Virtues** is the judicial act of **Pre-emptive Encapsulation**. It is the process of moving your child's spiritual assets specifically their Wealth Capacity, their Creative Fire, and their Vitality into a **Kingdom Trust** where the enemy cannot reach them. You are "Locking In" their success before the world has a chance to offer its "Illegal Exchanges."

**Locking in Wealth: The "Covenant of the Flourishing Seed"**

Wealth in the Kingdom is not just money; it is the **Power to Get Wealth** (Deuteronomy 8:18).

**The "Ant Thievery" Clause:** Many young adults enter the workforce and immediately encounter "Devourerers" bad investments, predatory lenders, or a spirit of "Pocket with Holes."

**The Secure Asset:** By "Locking in Wealth" now, you are legislating for a **Perpetual Surplus**. You are decreeing that their "Earning Frequency" is set to Kingdom Standards before they ever receive their first paycheck. You are placing a "Hedge of Protection" over their future bank accounts.

To explain **Locking in Wealth**, we must shift from the natural view of "making money" to the spiritual reality of **Financial Stature**. In the Kingdom, wealth is a "Covenant Technology." It is not about the currency in the hand, but the **"Magnetism of the Seed."** By locking this in now, you are ensuring that your children do not just "find jobs," but that they carry an "Atmosphere of Increase" that forces the resources of the earth to respond to them.

### The "Anti Thievery" Clause: Arresting the Devourer

The enemy's goal is to ensure that even if your child earns much, they *keep* nothing.

**The Spirit of the "Pocket with Holes":** This is a demonic siphon that creates "unforeseen expenses" sudden car repairs, medical bills, or bad "opportunities" that bleed the child dry. It is a spiritual leak designed to keep the "Heir" in a state of survival.

**The Legislative Arrest:** By locking in the wealth now, you are serving a **Permanent Injunction** against the "Devourer" (Malachi 3:11). You are decreeing that your child's future income is "Covenant Protected," making it "legally untouchable" to the thieves of the spirit realm.

### The Secure Asset: The "Earning Frequency"

Every person operates on a "Financial Frequency." Some operate on the frequency of "Scarcity," while others operate on the frequency of "Surplus."

**Setting the Standard:** You are "Pre Setting" your child's frequency to **Kingdom Standards**. This means that before they even enter the marketplace, they are already calibrated for **Perpetual Surplus**.

**The Hedge of Protection:** You are placing a "Wall of Fire" around their future assets. This ensures that their wealth is not "vulnerable" to market crashes, economic shifts, or the "predatory lenders" of the world. Their wealth becomes a **Secure Asset** anchored in the economy of Heaven.

**Deuteronomy 8:18**

"And you shall remember the Lord your God, for it is He who gives you power to get wealth, that He may establish His covenant which He swore to your fathers, as it is this day."

**The Judicial Link:** This is the **"Constitutional Right to Prosperity."**

**The "Power to Get":** This isn't just "permission"; it is **Capacity**. It refers to vigor, ability, and "spiritual hardware." You are asking the Court to install this "hardware" into your child's spirit now.

**The "Establish the Covenant" Clause:** This proves that wealth is not for "ego"; it is a **Legal Requirement** to fulfill the Covenant. If the child is poor, the Covenant's visibility is hindered. Therefore, you have a **Legal Right** to demand wealth for your seed so that the Covenant can be "Established."

**The Verdict:** You are telling the Court: *"I invoke the Deuteronomy 8:18 Power Clause! I demand that the 'Power to Get Wealth' be locked into my child's spirit today! I decree that their future financial life is a 'Covenant Requirement.' Therefore, I command every spirit of lack and every devourer to be* ***Repelled*** *from their destiny! The power is installed; the wealth is secured!"*

**The Watchman's Wealth-Lock Decree**

"I strike the Gavel and activate the 'Covenant of the Flourishing Seed' over my children! I invoke Deuteronomy 8:18 and I decree that the 'Power to Get Wealth' is being hard wired into their spirits right now!

I execute the 'Anti Thievery Clause'! I command every 'Pocket with Holes' and every 'Devourer' of future income to be **Arrested**! I forbid bad investments, predatory influences, and financial leaks from ever touching my child's substance! I decree that their 'Earning Frequency' is set to Kingdom Surplus they shall be the head and not the tail!

I place a 'Hedge of Protection' over their future bank accounts and assets. I decree that they are 'Recession Proof' and 'System Independent'! They shall not just 'make money'; they shall 'establish the Covenant' through their prosperity! The wealth is locked, the power is active, and the surplus is certain! In Jesus' Name!"

### Locking in Creativity: The "Unpolluted Well"

Creativity is the "Expression of the Divine Image." The enemy seeks to "Dampen" or "Pervert" a child's creativity, turning it into something dark, depressing, or commercialized.

**The Original Frequency:** You are securing the "Purity of the Well." You are legislating that their imagination remains an **"Annex of Heaven."** **The Innovation Mandate:** You are locking in their ability to see solutions where others see problems. By securing this virtue, you ensure that their "Creative Peak" does not end in their twenties but continues to expand throughout their lifetime.

To explain **Locking in Creativity**, we must view the imagination not as a playground, but as a **Spiritual Portal**. Creativity is the "Birth Right of the Image of God." It is the ability to pull things from the "Unseen" and manifest them in the "Seen." When you lock this virtue in, you are ensuring that the "Well" of your child's imagination remains un poisoned by the dark frequencies of the world's culture.

### The Original Frequency: The "Annex of Heaven"

The world's system seeks to "Capture" a child's imagination and harness it for "Dark Expression" (art that celebrates despair) or "Perversion" (art that mocks the Divine).

**Securing the Purity:** By legislating for the **"Unpolluted Well,"** you are decreeing that your child's mind is a **"Sanctified Territory."** You are telling the spirit realm: *"Only the patterns, colors, and sounds of Heaven are authorized to land in this imagination."*

**The Shielded Vision:** You are creating a firewall against "Creative Dampening", the spirit that makes a child "dull" or "robotic." You are ensuring they retain their **"Original Wonder."**

**The Innovation Mandate: Solutions as a Service**

Kingdom creativity is more than "Art"; it is **Spiritual Problem Solving**.

**Seeing the Unseen:** The "Innovation Mandate" is the ability to look at a chaotic situation and see the "Hidden Solution." This is the spirit of Joseph in Egypt or Daniel in Babylon.

**The Perpetual Peak:** Most people have a "Creative Peak" that fades. By "Locking in" this virtue, you are legislating for **Spiritual Elasticity**. You are decreeing that their best ideas will not come at 25, but will continue to grow in "Sharpness" and "Scope" as they age.

**Exodus 31:3**

"And I have filled him with the Spirit of God, in wisdom, in understanding, in knowledge, and in all manner of workmanship."

**The Judicial Link:** This is the **"Statute of the Master Craftsman."**

**Filled with the Spirit (*Ruwach*):** This proves that high level creativity is a **Spiritual Impartation**, not just a natural talent. It is the "Filling" that protects the well from pollution.

**All Manner of Workmanship:** This covers everything from technology and architecture to music and strategy. It is the **Legal Authorization** for diverse creative expression.

**The Verdict:** You are telling the Court: *"I invoke the Bezaleel Anointing of Exodus 31! I demand that my child be 'Filled' with this Spirit now! I decree that their imagination is 'Reserved' for the workmanship of the Kingdom! I 'Lock In' their wisdom and understanding so that no 'Spirit of Darkness' can occupy their creative faculty. Their mind is an Annex of Heaven, and their well is **Unpolluted!**"*

**The Watchman's Creative Lock Decree**

"I strike the Gavel and enter a 'Sanctification Order' over my child's imagination! I invoke Exodus 31:3 and I decree that my seed is **'Filled'** with the Spirit of God in all wisdom and workmanship!

I 'Lock In' the Purity of the Well! I forbid every spirit of depression, perversion, and darkness from landing in my child's creative space. I decree that their imagination is an 'Annex of Heaven'! I 'Jam the Signal' of ungodly culture and I command their 'Original Frequency' to remain sharp and clear!

I activate the 'Innovation Mandate'! I decree that they shall see solutions where the world sees crisis! I 'Lock In' their Creative Momentum; I command their Peak to be Perpetual! They shall not 'Burn Out' or 'Dry Up'; they shall be 'Ever Flowing' Wells of Divine Expression! The mind is secured, the well is pure, and the innovation is authorized! In Jesus' Name!"

**Locking in Longevity: The "Law of the Full Number"**

The enemy uses "Premature Exit" (accidents, chronic illness, or lifestyle traps) to cut a destiny short.

**The Full Harvest:** Longevity is the legal right to stay on the earth until your "Volume of the Book" is finished.

**The Life Extension Decree:** You are "Locking In" the **Health of the Cells** and the **Safety of the Path**. You are decreeing that no "Assigned Death" or "Ancestral Expiration Date" can touch your seed. They shall not "wither" in their prime; they shall flourish until their mandate is complete.

To explain **Locking in Longevity**, we must understand that in the Kingdom, life is not a "random duration" but a **"Contractual Term."** Every child comes to earth with a specific "Volume of the Book" (Psalm 40:7) to fulfill. The enemy's strategy is **"Foreclosure by Premature Exit"** attempting to evict the spirit from the body before the assignment is complete. Locking in longevity is the judicial act of securing the "Full Number" of their days.

### The Full Harvest: The Legal Right to Finish

Longevity is not just about "being old"; it is about **Mandate Completion**.

**The Volume of the Book:** Every destiny has a "Page Count." If a child's assignment requires 80 years but they are taken at 40, the Kingdom suffers a **"Productivity Deficit."**

**The Judicial Right:** You are legislating for your child's right to stay on the earth until every "Prophetic Sentence" written about them has been lived out. You are decreeing: *"This life cannot be truncated! The harvest must be full!"*

### 2. The Life Extension Decree: Neutralizing the "Expiration Date"

The enemy often uses "Ancestral Expiration Dates" patterns where men or women in a family die at a specific age to set a "Timer" on your child's life.

**Health of the Cells:** You are "Locking In" the biological integrity of their body. You are decreeing that their "Biological Clock" is governed by the Spirit, not by "bloodline glitches" or chronic infirmities.

**Safety of the Path:** This is the **"Anti Accident Clause."** You are legislating that their "Going Out and Coming In" is shielded from the "lifestyle traps" (addiction, risky behavior) and "assigned deaths" (accidents, violence) that the enemy uses to "snatch" a destiny.

**Exodus 23:26**

"No one shall suffer miscarriage or be barren in your land; I will fulfill the number of your days."

**The Judicial Link:** This is the **"Statute of the Guaranteed Term."**

**No Miscarriage/Barrenness:** In the spirit, this refers to **Destiny Abortion.** It is a decree that nothing started in your child's life will be cut off before it reaches maturity.
**"I Will Fulfill":** To "fill to the brim" or "to satisfy a requirement." It is a **Sovereign Guarantee** that the "Number" of their days is not subject to negotiation with the enemy.
**The Verdict:** You are telling the Court: *"I invoke the Exodus 23:26 Guarantee! I demand that the 'Number of Days' for my seed be **Filled To The Brim**! I strike down every 'Ancestral Timer' and every 'Premature Exit' strategy! I decree that my child is 'Inhabiting the Fullness' of their term. They shall not wither; they shall finish the Book! The number is set, and the Lord shall fulfill it!"*

### The Watchman's Longevity-Lock Decree

"I strike the Gavel and execute the 'Law of the Full Number' over my seed! I invoke Exodus 23:26 and I decree that the Lord is fulfilling the number of my children's days! I 'Lock In' their vitality and I 'Seal' their biological integrity!

I 'Deactivate' every Ancestral Expiration Date! I decree that the 'Timer of the Enemy' is **Broken**! My children shall not die in their prime; they shall not wither in the 'Morning' of their destiny! I cancel every 'Assigned Death,' every 'Scheduled Accident,' and every 'Lifestyle Trap' designed to cut their Volume short!

I decree 'Health to their Cells' and 'Safety to their Path'! They are the 'Long Distance Runners' of the Kingdom! They shall stay on this earth until every word written in their 'Volume' is performed! They shall see their children's children and walk in the 'Full Harvest' of their days! The Number is **Secured;** the Exit is **Cancelled**! In Jesus' Name!"

**Psalm 121:7-8**

"The Lord shall preserve you from all evil; He shall preserve your soul. The Lord shall preserve your going out and your coming in from this time forth, and even forevermore."

**The Judicial Link:** This is the **"Statute of Perpetual Preservation."**

**The "From This Time Forth" Clause:** This is the **Lock In Activation**. It establishes a "Starting Point" for the security system.

**The "Going Out and Coming In":** This refers to their "Transactions" (Wealth), their "Movements" (Longevity), and their "Expressions" (Creativity).

**The Verdict:** You are telling the Court: *"I invoke the Preservation Statute! I demand that my child's virtues be 'Preserved' from this moment forward! I place their future wealth, their creative essence, and their physical life into the 'Forevermore' Vault of God. I decree a 'Lock In' that the world cannot break and the enemy cannot pick!"*

**The Watchman's Lock-In" Decree**

"I strike the Gavel and enter the 'Vault of the Covenant' over my seed! I invoke Psalm 121:7-8 and I decree that the Lord is the PRESERVER of my child's virtues! I 'Lock In' their Wealth, their Creativity, and their Longevity NOW!

I decree that my child is 'Redeemed from Poverty' before they ever encounter a struggle! I lock in the 'Power to Get Wealth' and I command every 'Devourer' to stay back from their future substance!

I secure the 'Well of Creativity' in their spirit! I decree that their imagination is a 'Sacred Territory' that shall never be polluted or commercialized by the world! I lock in their Longevity; I cancel every 'Ancestral Expiration Date' and every 'Scheduled Accident.' I decree they shall fulfill the 'Full Number' of their days in strength and vitality!

I move their virtues into the 'Kingdom Trust.' I seal the vault with the Blood of Jesus! From this time forth and even forevermore, my children are **Preserved, Protected**, and **Perpetually Productive!** The Gavel has fallen; the virtues are locked! In Jesus' Name!"

## Chapter 14: The Power of Consistency

### *Preventing Addictions and Soul Ties Through Disciplined Prayer*

In the spiritual realm, **Consistency** is not just a habit; it is a **"Force Field."** The enemy rarely attempts to breach a destiny with one massive blow; instead, he uses the "Law of Attrition" small, repeated compromises that eventually wear down a child's resistance.

**Disciplined Prayer** is the judicial act of **Environmental Maintenance**. It ensures that the "Spiritual Atmosphere" surrounding your child remains too pressurized for the "Parasites" of addiction and unholy soul ties to latch on. Consistency turns your prayer from a "one time event" into a **"Permanent Infrastructure."**

### Preventing Addictions: Breaking the "Dopamine Trap"

Addiction is more than a chemical dependency; it is a **"Spiritual Siphon."** It is the enemy's attempt to replace the "Joy of the Lord" with a "Counterfeit Ecstasy."

**The Frequency of Peace:** Consistent prayer sets a "Baseline Frequency" in the home. When a child is raised in an atmosphere of consistent prayer, their spirit becomes accustomed to **"High Level Peace."**

**The Repulsion Factor:** A spirit that is "Full of the Ghost" finds the "Heavy Frequency" of addiction repulsive. By being consistent, you are pre emptively "Immunizing" your child's brain chemistry against the hooks of substance abuse, digital dependency, and secret habits. You are decreeing: *"My child's appetite is reserved for the Divine; there is no vacancy for the artificial!"*

To explain **Breaking the "Dopamine Trap,"** we must understand that addiction is a **Displacement of Worship**. The brain's reward system was designed by God to find "Ecstasy" in His

Presence and "Satisfaction" in His Purpose. The enemy attempts to hijack this "Internal Altar" by installing a "Counterfeit Frequency" that binds the soul to a physical or digital substance.

Preventing addiction through consistent prayer is the judicial act of **"Pre-empting the Altar."** You are filling the "Reward Centers" of your child's soul with the Light of God before the world has a chance to fill them with darkness.

**The Frequency of Peace: Establishing the "Baseline"**

Every household operates on a "Baseline Frequency." In many homes, the baseline is stress, noise, or digital distraction.

**The High-level Peace:** Consistent prayer creates a **"Stabilized Atmosphere."** When a child's spirit is conditioned to the "High Level Peace" of the Holy Spirit, their internal "tuning fork" is set to a frequency of tranquility and joy.

**The Detection of "Noise":** Because their baseline is Peace, they will immediately feel the "Static" of ungodly influences. They will be able to sense when a digital game, a social media app, or a "secret habit" is trying to lower their frequency. The Peace acts as a **Natural Alarm System**.

**The Repulsion Factor: Spiritual Immunity**

In physics, two objects cannot occupy the same space at the same time. In the spirit, the soul "Full of the Ghost" has **No Vacancy** for the artificial.

**Brain Chemistry Immunization:** By praying consistently over your child, you are legislating for their **"Neuro Spiritual Integrity."** You are decreeing that their brain's neural pathways are "Kingdom Property."

**The "Heavy Frequency" of Addiction:** Addiction carries a "Low, Dense Frequency" that feels like a weight. A spirit accustomed to the "Lightness of Glory" will find the "Heaviness of the Hook" repulsive. They won't just "resist" the addiction; they will find it **unpalatable**. Their appetite will be "Reserved for the Divine."

**Breaking the Siphon: Safeguarding the Joy**

Addiction is a "Siphon" because it drains the child's "Natural Joy" to power a "Demonic High." Consistent prayer acts as a **Check Valve**. It ensures that the "Joy of the Lord" remains the child's strength, preventing the "Leakage" that leads to the search for a counterfeit.

**Psalm 16:11**

"You will show me the path of life; In Your presence is fullness of joy; At Your right hand are pleasures forevermore."

**The Judicial Link:** This is the **"Statute of the Superior Pleasure."**

**The "Fullness of Joy" Clause:** The word "Fullness" means "satisfaction" or "surfeit." It is the legal argument that the human soul can only be "satisfied" by the Presence. Everything else is a "Partial" that leads to addiction.

**The "Pleasures Forevermore"** This proves that "Kingdom High" is **Sustainable**, unlike the "Worldly High" which is temporary and destructive.

**The Verdict:** You are telling the Court: *"I invoke the Psalm 16:11 Statute! I decree that my child's soul is satisfied ONLY by the Fullness of Joy found in the Presence! I 'Void' every counterfeit pleasure and every dopamine trap! I demand that my child be 'Immunized' by the Superior Pleasure of the Right Hand of God! The 'Artificial' has no room; the 'Divine' has taken the Altar! The siphon is broken, and the joy is* ***Secured!****"*

**The Watchman's Anti-Addiction Decree**

"I strike the Gavel and legislate for the 'Neuro Spiritual Integrity' of my seed! I invoke Psalm 16:11 and I decree that my child is 'Saturated' with the Fullness of Joy that comes only from the Presence of God!

I execute the 'Repulsion Factor' over their brain chemistry! I decree that my child's neural pathways are 'Holy Ground.' I forbid every spirit of addiction, every digital hook, and every secret habit from forming a 'stronghold' in their reward system! I command their 'Appetite' to be reserved for the Divine!

I establish a 'Baseline Frequency of Peace' in this home! I decree that the 'Artificial' is repulsive to my children! I 'Plug the Leak' of their joy and I command every 'Spiritual Siphon' to be dismantled! My child shall not seek the 'Counterfeit Ecstasy' of the world, for they are already 'Drunk on the New Wine' of the Spirit! The altar is occupied; the trap is broken! In Jesus' Name!"

### Preventing Soul Ties: The "Sovereign Soul" Decree

A soul tie is an **"Unauthorized Link"** between your child's heart and a person or system that is not aligned with their destiny. These ties are often formed through shared trauma, ungodly intimacy, or intense peer pressure.

**The "Clean Border" Protocol:** Consistent, disciplined prayer acts like a **"Border Patrol"** for your child's emotions. It constantly "scrubs" their soul of lingering influences.

**Preserving Autonomy:** You are legislating for a **"Sovereign Soul."** This means your child remains "whole" and "unfragmented." By praying consistently, you are preventing the enemy from "weaving" your child's destiny into the "web" of another person's dysfunction. You are cutting the strings before they become knots.

To explain the **"Sovereign Soul" Decree**, we must understand that the soul is intended to be a **Unitary Vessel** fully intact and exclusively linked to its Creator. In the spirit, a "Soul Tie" acts as a **Demonic Bridge** or a "Shared Circuit" where the trauma, dysfunction, and "iniquity patterns" of another person can flow directly into your child’s life.

By legislating for a **Sovereign Soul**, you are ensuring that your child’s identity remains un diluted and their destiny remains "un hitched" from the sinking ships of ungodly associations.

### The "Clean Border" Protocol: Atmospheric Scrubbing

Every person your child interacts with leaves a "Spiritual Residue." If left unchecked, this residue becomes a "Foothold."

**The Emotional Border Patrol:** Consistent, disciplined prayer acts as a **"Sanitization Sweep."** It identifies and "washes off" the ungodly influences of peer pressure, manipulative teachers, or toxic friends before they can penetrate the "Inner Court" of the soul.

**The "Scrubbing" Effect:** Just as a physical wound must be cleaned to prevent infection, your daily prayer "scrubs" the child's soul of "lingering frequencies" from the day. It ensures that when they sleep, their soul is **"Reset to Zero"** linked only to God.

### Preserving Autonomy: Preventing the "Web"

The enemy’s goal is to "fragment" the soul. He wants to "weave" your child’s future into a "Web of Dysfunction" by linking them to someone who is headed for destruction.

**The Unfragmented Soul:** A "Sovereign Soul" is a **Whole Soul**. It means your child doesn't "leave a piece of themselves" in every relationship or environment.

**Cutting the Strings:** Disciplined prayer identifies the "invisible threads" of manipulation or ungodly soul attachment early. You are **"Cutting the Strings before they become Knots."** You are legislating that your child’s "Emotional Equity" cannot be traded or stolen by another person’s needs or demands.

**Psalms 124:7**

"Our soul has escaped as a bird from the snare of the fowlers; the snare is broken, and we have escaped."

**The Judicial Link:** This is the **"Statute of the Broken Snare."**

**The "Bird" and the "Snare":** A soul tie is a **"Snare"** it is designed to keep the "Bird" (the child's spirit) grounded.

**The "Broken" Clause:** The power of the soul tie lies in its **Connection**. Once the connection is "Broken" through judicial decree, the bird has "escaped." The snare still exists, but it has no power to *hold.*

**The Verdict:** You are telling the Court: *"I invoke the Psalm 124:7 Decree! I identify every 'Unauthorized Link' and every 'Fowler's Snare' targeting my child's soul. I command the snare to be BROKEN! I decree that my child's soul is 'Sovereign' and 'Autonomous.' Every ungodly weave and every toxic web is dissolved! My child has escaped! They are whole, they are free, and they are* ***Unfragmented!"***

## The Watchman's Sovereign Soul Decree

"I strike the Gavel and execute the 'Sovereign Soul Decree' over my seed! I invoke Psalm 124:7 and I declare that the snare is BROKEN and my child's soul has **Escaped!**

I activate the 'Clean Border Protocol'! I command the Holy Spirit to 'Scrub' my child's soul of every lingering influence, every ungodly word, and every 'Spiritual Residue' of peer pressure! I decree that their emotions are 'Holy Ground' and their heart is a 'No Go Zone' for ungodly ties!

I 'Legislate for Autonomy'! I forbid the enemy from 'weaving' my child's destiny into the web of another's dysfunction. I 'Cut the Strings' of every manipulative relationship and every unholy attachment before they can become knots!

I decree that my children are 'Whole and Unfragmented'! They shall not leave their 'Virtue' in the hands of the world! Their soul belongs to the King, their identity is anchored in Zion, and their destiny is 'Unreachable' from anything that is not of God! The Gavel has fallen; the soul is Sovereign! In Jesus' Name!"

**Disciplined Prayer: The "Pressure Cooker" Effect**

In physics, high pressure prevents boiling. In the spirit, a **High-Pressure Atmosphere of Prayer** prevents the "boiling over" of rebellion and lust.

**The Infrastructure of the Morning:** When you pray with discipline (at the same gates/times), you are building a **"Wall of Routine."** The enemy hates routine because he cannot find a "gap" in the schedule. Consistency closes the "Window of Opportunity" the enemy uses during times of boredom or spiritual laziness.

**Acts 6:4**

"But we will give ourselves continually to prayer and to the ministry of the word."

**The Judicial Link:** This is the **"Statute of Perpetual Devotion."**

**"Give Ourselves Continually":** Means to be "earnestly occupied with," "to adhere closely to," and "to be steadfastly attentive." It is the language of **Spiritual Tenacity**.

**The "Continual" Clause:** This proves that the power is not in the "loudness" of the prayer, but in its **Uninterrupted Flow**. It is the "Continual" nature of the prayer that builds the "Immunity."

**The Verdict:** You are telling the Court: *"I invoke the Acts 6:4 Protocol! I commit to the 'Continual' legislation of my child's future! I decree that because of this consistency, a 'Permanent Fence' is built around their soul. I demand that every addiction and every unholy soul tie be 'Starved' of entry! The atmosphere is too thick for the enemy to breathe! The decree is continual, and the protection is* ***Perpetual!"***

**The Watchman's Consistency Decree**

"I strike the Gavel and activate the 'Power of Consistency' over my seed! I invoke Acts 6:4 and I decree that I am 'Steadfastly Attentive' to the spiritual borders of my home!

I execute the 'Anti Addiction Mandate'! I decree that my child's spirit and brain chemistry are 'Immunized' against every ungodly hook and every counterfeit ecstasy! I command their 'Appetites' to be aligned with the Kingdom. I forbid the 'Dopamine Trap' from catching my seed!

I legislate for a 'Sovereign Soul'! I cut every 'Unauthorized Link' and every 'Unholy Soul Tie' before it can form! I decree that my child is 'Whole' and 'Unfragmented.' I command the 'Border Patrol' of the Holy Spirit to guard their heart from every toxic connection and every peer driven web!

I build a 'Wall of Routine' around their destiny! I decree that because of my disciplined prayer, there is **No Gap** for the enemy to enter! The atmosphere of this home is 'High Pressure' and 'Glory Filled'! The parasites of darkness cannot survive here! Consistency is my weapon, and Victory is our permanent state! In Jesus' Name!"

## Chapter 15: From The Nursery to The Nation

### *How a Stable, Praying Home Heals the World*

In the architecture of the Kingdom, the home is not a "secluded bunker"; it is a **Power Plant.** The atmosphere you have cultivated the locked in virtues, the severed lineage traps, and the wall of fire does not stay within your four walls. It begins to "leak" into the geography around you.

**From the Nursery to the Nation** is the judicial realization that the "Gavel of the Mother" is actually a **Legislative Instrument for National Transformation**. When you heal the seed in the nursery, you are essentially "curing" the future leadership of the nation.

**The "Epicenter" Effect: The Home as a Spiritual Hub**

A stable, praying home creates a **"Geographical Shift." The Atmospheric Radius:** Just as a radio tower broadcasts a signal over a certain radius, a "Zion Class" home broadcasts the frequency of Peace and Order. Neighbors, schools, and local systems begin to "inhale" the surplus of the Glory that you have generated.

**Healing the Soil:** By dealing with the "Marine Spirits" and "Ancestral Infirmities" in your own lineage, you are actually "clearing the air" for the entire community. You are a **"Cultural Carrier"** you carry the "antibodies" of the Kingdom into a "sick" world.

To explain the **"Epicenter" Effect**, we must move beyond the idea of prayer as a private conversation and see it as a **Spiritual Broadcast**. In the Kingdom, a consecrated home is a "High Pressure Zone" of the Spirit. Just as weather systems move from areas of high pressure to low pressure, the "Atmosphere of Zion" created in your home naturally seeks to expand and displace the "Low Pressure" systems of chaos, fear, and disorder in your surrounding geography.

### The Atmospheric Radius: The "Zion Class" Broadcast

A stable, praying home functions like a **Spiritual Radio Tower.**

**The Frequency of Order:** When you legislate "Order" in your nursery, you are broadcasting a frequency that stabilizes the "tectonic plates" of your neighborhood.

**Spiritual Inhalation:** People who enter your "Atmospheric Radius" whether they are neighbors, delivery drivers, or houseguests begin to "inhale" the surplus of Peace you have generated. They may not understand the theology, but they will experience the **Relief**. You are creating a "Sanctuary Zone" where the demonic "Static" of the city is silenced.

### Healing the Soil: The "Antibody" Protocol

In many regions, the "Soil" (the spiritual history of the land) is contaminated by "Marine Spirits" (spirits of lust, confusion, and instability) or "Ancestral Infirmities" (generational poverty or sickness).

**The Cultural Carrier:** As you deal with these spirits in your own bloodline, you develop **"Spiritual Antibodies."** You become a carrier of the "Cure."

**Clearing the Air:** When you "evict" a spirit of addiction from your home, you weaken its grip on your entire street. You are "Clearing the Air" for the community, making it easier for others to breathe, believe, and break free. You are not just a resident; you are a **Geographical Sanctifier**.

**Mathew 5:14**

"You are the light of the world. A city that is set on a hill cannot be hidden."

**The Judicial Link:** This is the **"Statute of Visibility and Influence."**

**"City Set on a Hill":** This refers to the **Elevation of Atmosphere**. A "Zion Class" home is spiritually "Elevated" above the "Lowlands" of the world's system.

**"Cannot Be Hidden":** This is a **Judicial Guarantee**. It means that the "Light" (the Glory) you generate is legally required to affect the "Darkness" around it. The darkness has no legal standing to "extinguish" your broadcast; it can only be "displaced" by it.

**The Verdict:** You are telling the Court: *"I invoke the 'City on a Hill' Statute! I decree that my home is a 'Geographical Epicenter' of the Kingdom! I demand that the frequency of Peace generated in this house be 'Broadcast' across my neighborhood! I declare that the 'Soil' of this community is being 'Healed' by the antibodies of my lineage! My home is a Lighthouse, and the darkness MUST recede! The signal is clear; the shift is manifest!"*

### The Watchman's Epicenter Decree

"I strike the Gavel and authorize the 'Broadcast of Zion' from this property! I invoke Matthew 5:14 and I decree that my home is a 'City on a Hill' that **Cannot** be hidden! I 'Set the Frequency' of this entire block to the Peace and Order of the Kingdom!

"I activate the 'Antibody Protocol' over my neighborhood! Because I have dealt with the 'Marine Spirits' and 'Ancestral Infirmities' in my own blood, I now 'Clear the Air' for my community! I decree that every 'Spiritual Pollutant' over this street is being neutralized by the Glory of my household!

"I decree that my home is a 'Spiritual Hub'! I command every system the schools, the businesses, and the local government to 'Inhale' the Surplus of the Spirit generated in my 'Nursery'! We are the 'Cultural Carriers' of the New Nation! The soil is healed, the atmosphere is stabilized, and the Light of God is our permanent signal! In Jesus' Name!"

**The Exportation of Character: Raising "System Healers"**

The world is currently in a state of "Systemic Collapse" because the "Cells" (individuals) are broken.

**The Healed Heir:** When your child leaves the "Deliverance Lab" of your home, they enter the world not as a "victim" of the culture, but as a **"Systemic Disruptor." The National Antidote:** Because they have "Locked in Integrity" and "Unpolluted Creativity," they don't just "survive" in a corporation or a government; they **Sanitize** it. One child, raised under the Gavel of a Watchman Mother, can "Heal a Nation" by introducing a frequency of righteousness that was previously missing.

To explain the **Exportation of Character**, we must view the child not as a "graduate" of a home, but as a **"Biological Antidote"** being released into a contaminated system. In the Kingdom, a child who has been raised in a "Deliverance Lab" where virtues are locked and lineages are cleansed becomes a carrier of **"Incorruptible Seed."** When they enter a "broken" system (politics, business, or education), they don't just "do a job"; they **Sanitize the Environment** by their very presence.

**The Healed Heir: The "Systemic Disruptor"**

Most individuals enter the world's systems as "Victims" of the culture they are molded by the corruption, anxiety, and greed of the environment because they have no "internal firewall."

**The Disruptor Protocol:** A "Healed Heir" enters as a **Disruptor**. Because they carry a "Higher Frequency" of peace and integrity, they do not "blend in." Their presence creates a "Spiritual Friction" against corruption.

**The Immunity to "Group Think":** Because you have "Locked in" their creativity and identity, they are immune to the "Collective Madness" of the age. They don't just follow the "corporate manual"; they rewrite it according to the **"Original Patterns of Heaven."**

**The National Antidote: Sanitizing the System**

A nation is simply a collection of systems (government, media, family, religion, etc.). When these systems "collapse," it is because the "Cells" (the people) are carrying the "viruses" of dishonesty and compromise.

**The One Child Mandate:** It only takes **one** sanitized cell to begin the healing of an organ. One child, raised under the "Gavel of a Watchman Mother," enters a corporation or a government office and introduces a **"Frequency of Righteousness." The Sanitation Effect:** Their "Locked in Integrity" acts like a **Spiritual Bleach**. Dark agendas, secret deals, and oppressive atmospheres cannot survive long in the proximity of a child who breathes the "Atmosphere of the Glory." They heal the nation by **recalibrating** every system they touch.

**Genesis 41:38-39**

"And Pharaoh said to his servants, 'Can we find such a one as this, a man in whom is the Spirit of God?' Then Pharaoh said to Joseph, 'Inasmuch as God has shown you all this, there is no one as discerning and wise as you.'"

**The Judicial Link:** This is the **"Statute of the Indispensable Heir."**

**The "Such a One" Clause:** This refers to the **Uniqueness of Character**. Joseph was a "System Healer" who entered a pagan government and "Sanitized" the economy of the world.

**"No One as Discerning":** This is the result of the "Unpolluted Well" (Creativity). Because his well was pure, Joseph could see solutions that the "World's Experts" could not see.

**The Verdict:** You are telling the Court: *"I invoke the Joseph Mandate over my seed! I decree that my child is a 'System Healer' for this nation! I demand that wherever they walk into boardrooms, courtrooms, or classrooms they carry the 'Spirit of God' that Pharaoh recognized! I decree that they shall* *not be 'Infected' by the system, but they shall 'Sanitize' it! One child, under the Gavel, is enough to heal a nation! The Antidote is released!"*

### The Watchman's "System-healer" Decree

"I strike the Gavel and authorize the 'Exportation of Character' from this Nursery to the Nation! I invoke Genesis 41:38 and I decree that my children are the 'Josephs' of this generation men and women in whom is the Spirit of God!

"I decree that my seed is a 'Systemic Disruptor'! They shall not be victims of the culture; they shall be the **Architects** of the New Kingdom Culture! I release them as 'Biological Antidotes' into every corrupted system! I command their 'Locked in Integrity' to act as a 'Spiritual Bleach' everywhere they go!

"I decree that their 'Unpolluted Creativity' provides solutions for national crises! They shall not 'Survive' in the world; they shall 'Sanitize' it! I command every 'Pharaoh' in their future to recognize the Light they carry! I decree that one child from this house is enough to 'Recalibrate' the frequency of this nation! The Antidote is active, the System is being healed, and the Glory is manifest! In Jesus' Name!"

### The "Restoration of the Foundations"

The Bible says that if the foundations are destroyed, what can the righteous do? The answer is: **They rebuild them in the Nursery. Generational Legislation:** Every time you pray for your child's consistency, you are "voting" for a stable future society. You are legislating against the "National Addictions" and "National Debt" by ensuring your own seed is free from them. The nursery is the "Foundry" where the new foundation of the nation is cast.

**Isaiah 58:12**

"Those from among you shall build the old waste places; you shall raise up the foundations of many generations; and you shall be called the Repairer of the Breach, the Restorer of Streets to Dwell In."

**The Judicial Link:** This is the **"Statute of the Master Rebuilder."**

**"Those From Among You":** This refers to your **Seed**. The "Builders" are the children you have raised in the "Deliverance Lab."

**"Foundations of Many Generations":** This proves that the work you do in the nursery has **"Multi-Generational Reach."** You aren't just praying for a "good kid"; you are raising a "Foundation."

**The Verdict:** You are telling the Court: *"I invoke the Isaiah 58:12 Mandate! I decree that my seed are the 'Repairers of the Breach'! I refuse to believe that the world is 'too far gone.' I present my stable, praying home as the 'Laboratory of Restoration.' From this nursery, I release the 'Builders' of the next nation! I decree that the 'Waste Places' of my city and my country shall be rebuilt by the hands of my heirs!"*

**The Watchman's Global Impact Decree**

"I strike the Gavel and authorize the 'Exportation of Glory' from this home to the Nations! I invoke Isaiah 58:12 and I decree that my children are the 'Repairers of the Breach' and the 'Restorers of the Streets'!

I decree that my home is an 'Epicenter of National Healing'! The Peace we have cultivated here shall 'Leak' into our schools, our workplaces, and our government! I forbid the 'Pollutants of the Age' from entering my home, and I command the 'Antidote of the Kingdom' to leave my home and saturate the world!

I release 'System Healers' into the earth! I decree that my seed shall not be 'Conformed' to the world, but they shall 'Transform' it by the frequency of their character! They are the 'New Foundations' upon which the next generation shall stand!

I declare that the 'Gavel of the Mother' has spoken: The nursery is healed, and therefore the **Nation Is Healed**! The breach is repaired, the streets are restored, and the Glory of the Lord is our **Rear Guard**! In Jesus' Name!"

## Conclusion: Arise, O Mother of Lions!

### The Final Charge to Occupy the Gate

The term "Mother of Lions" is a **Judicial Rank**. In the spirit, a lion does not beg for territory; it occupies it. To "Arise" is to shift from domestic duty to **High Level Governance**. You are the guardian of the "Lion's Pride," and your roar is the **Gavel Strike** of Heaven.

### 1. The Nature of the "Lioness" Anointing

As the **Operational Commander**, the lioness secures the environment for the next generation. Your love is now **Strategic and Sovereign**.

**The Calculated Watch:** You are no longer praying "blanket prayers." You are a **Watchman** identifying the "Siphons" (leaks in focus) and "Parasites" (ungodly habits) to pre-emptively close every gate.

**The Territorial Roar:** Your decree is a **Frequency of Ownership**. It informs the atmosphere that this lineage is **Occupied**. It acts as a "No Trespassing" sign to scavengers and marine spirits.

**Amos 3:8**

*"A lion has roared; Who will not fear? The Lord God has spoken; Who can but prophesy?"*

**The Verdict:** You are invoking the **Statute of Irresistible Authority**. When you roar, the spirit realm is legally required to respond with "Reverence and Retreat."

**2. Occupying the Gate: The Seat of Authority**

Whoever controls the **Gate** controls the city. By taking your seat, you become the **Sovereign Filter** of your home.

**The Legislative Seat:** As the **Chief Justice**, you issue the **Primary Verdict** on your children's identity. You don't wait for "trends"; you rule that they are Kings, Priests, and Holy Seed.

**The Filter of Zion:** You are the **Border Patrol**. You stand at the gates of their eyes, ears, and minds to "Search and Seize" contraband ideologies that do not carry the Seal of the King**Psalm 127:5**

*"Happy is the man who has his quiver full of them... they shall speak with their enemies in the gate."*

- **The Verdict:** You are invoking the **Statute of the Confrontational Gate**. When the enemy "sues" for your child's destiny, you meet them with a Superior Decree that silences every claim.

**3. The Charge: From Defense to Dominion**

Stop praying "survival" prayers; start praying **Dominion** prayers. You are raising **Architects**, not just inhabitants.

**THE LION'S MANIFESTO**

**Genesis 49:9 (Statute of Rest):** Your seed shall be so authoritative that the enemy finds it "too dangerous" to rouse or disturb their peace.

**Ezekiel 19:2 (Statute of Environment):** You cannot raise a lion in a sheepfold. You must "lay down among lions" (the Word and the Glory) so your children inherit the **DNA of Boldness**.

**Genesis 22:17 (Statute of Offensive Warfare):** Your descendants are destined to **Possess the Enemy's Gate** taking over the boardrooms, courtrooms, and systems of government.

**The Watchman's Consolidated Decrees**

**The Territorial Roar**

"I strike the Gavel and release the 'Territorial Roar' over my children! I invoke Amos 3:8 and broadcast the 'Frequency of Ownership'! I execute the 'Calculated Watch' and seal every gap with the Blood of the Lamb! I roar to every marine spirit: move on! This territory is occupied by the Glory of God! In Jesus' Name!"

**The Gate-Keeper**

"i take my seat at the Gate! I invoke Psalm 127:5 as the 'Chief Justice' of this household! I 'Veto' every cultural label and forbid 'Contraband Data' from entering my child's spirit! I 'Speak with the Enemy at the Gate' and command every demonic claim to be dismissed for lack of standing! The borders are tight! In Jesus' Name!"

**The Final Gavel Strike**

"I arise as a mother of Lions! I invoke Ezekiel 19:2; I am a Territorial Governor! I decree my seeds are 'Lion's Whelps' bold, fierce, and un-rousable! I activate the Genesis 22:17 Mandate: my descendants are possessing the gates of their enemies! They are the Apex Leaders of the New Kingdom Era! The Gavel has fallen, the Gate is occupied, and the Lion of Judah is our Rear Guard! ARISE!"

**The Governor's War Room: Prayer**

## I. THE LEGAL DEFEAT OF ANCESTRAL TRAPS

1. **Voiding the Illegal Exchange:** "By the blood of the everlasting covenant, I move for a **Spiritual Rescission** of every 'Life Altering Trap' set for my seed. Every 'Esau Syndrome' contract signed by my ancestors is now NULL and VOID." (**Hebrews 12:24**)

2. **Repossessing the 'Lent' Virtue:** "I strike the Gavel and command the return of every 'Star' and 'Gift' that was on loan to the kingdom of darkness. I decree that the 'Lease' is expired and the 'Writ of Repossession' is active." (**Joel 2:25**)

3. **Breaking the Siphon:** "I command every spiritual siphon attached to my child's brilliance or leadership to be shattered. The 'Siphoned Star' is returned to its original orbit." (**Isaiah 49:25**)

4. **Canceling Ancestral Expiration Dates:** "I de-activate every 'Timer of Death' and 'Scheduled Failure' in my bloodline. I decree that the 'Ancestral Expiration Date' is replaced by the **Law of the Full Number.**" (**Exodus 23:26**)

## II. THE LOCKING IN OF VIRTUES (CHAPTER 13)

5. **Wealth-Surplus Decree:** "I lock in the 'Power to Get Wealth' before my child enters the marketplace. I execute the **Anti-Thievery Clause** over their future income and assets." (**Deuteronomy 8:18**)

6. **Creativity Purity:** "I decree that my child's imagination is an **'Annex of Heaven.'** I lock in their creative frequency and forbid every 'Strange Fire' or demonic perversion from landing in their mind." (**Exodus 31:3**)

7. **Longevity Seal:** "I seal the 'Health of the Cells' and the 'Safety of the Path.' I decree that my seed shall not wither in their morning, but shall flourish until their **Volume of the Book** is complete." (**Psalm 91:16**)

8. **Consistency Power:** "I build a 'Wall of Routine' around my child's spiritual life. I decree that their consistency in prayer creates a 'Force Field' that the enemy cannot penetrate." (**Acts 6:4**)

## III. THE PRESERVATION OF THE SOUL (CHAPTER 14)

9. **Breaking the Dopamine Trap:** "I 'Immunize' my child's brain chemistry against every ungodly hook and addiction. I decree that their appetite is **Reserved for the Divine**." (**Psalm 16:11**)

10. **Sovereign Soul Decree:** "I cut every 'Unauthorized Link' and 'Ungodly Soul Tie' with the Sword of the Spirit. I decree that my child's soul is **Whole and Unfragmented**." (**Psalm 124:7**)

11. **Border Patrol of the Heart:** "I authorize the 'Clean Border Protocol' over my child's emotions. I command the Holy Spirit to 'Scrub' away every lingering influence of peer pressure or manipulation." (**Proverbs 4:23**)

12. **Anti-Rebellion Injunction:** "I issue a judicial injunction against the spirit of rebellion. I decree that my child's 'Ear' is circumcised to hear the frequency of Zion and ignore the noise of the world." (**Isaiah 50:4**)

## IV. THE GATE-KEEPER'S DOMINION (CHAPTER 15)

13. **Occupying the Gate:** "I take my seat as the **Chief Justice** of my home. I 'Veto' every cultural agenda that attempts to define my seed. My verdict of 'Holy Identity' stands." (**Psalm 127:5**)

14. **The Epicenter Shift:** "I decree that my home is a **'Zion Class' Spiritual Hub.** The frequency of Peace generated in my nursery is now healing the soil of my community." (**Matthew 5:14**)

15. **System Healer Activation:** "I release my children as **'Biological Antidotes'** into the systems of this nation. Wherever they walk, they sanitize the environment and introduce the Order of God." (**Genesis 41:38**)

16. **The Joseph Mandate:** "I decree that my seed shall possess 'Superior Wisdom' that makes them indispensable to governments

and corporations. They are the **Repairers of the Breach.**" (**Isaiah 58:12**)

**V. THE ROAR OF THE LIONESS (CONCLUSION)**

17. **Territorial Roar:** "I release the Roar of the Lion of Judah through my decrees! I command every scavenger and monitoring spirit to MOVE ON! This lineage is **Occupied Territory.**" (**Amos 3:8**)

18. **Possessing the Enemy's Gate:** "I decree that my descendants shall not be 'Safe' inhabitants; they shall be **Aggressive Possessors** of the gates of their enemies." (**Genesis 22:17**)

19. **The Un Rousable Peace:** "I decree that my seed lies down like a 'Lion's Whelp.' I forbid the enemy from 'Rousing' or disturbing the peace of my household." (**Genesis 49:9**)

20. **Final Gavel Strike:** "I strike the Gavel and seal these prayers in the Courts of Heaven. What I have bound on earth is bound in spirit! The Nursery is healed, the Nation is shifting, and the Glory is manifest!" (**Matthew 18:18**)

**DECLARATIONS:**

1. "My nursery is not a daycare; it is a Legislative Assembly where the future of the nation is being decided."

2. "I am not just raising children; I am 'Programming the Frequency' of a lineage that will never know the taste of defeat."

3. "Every tear I shed in disciplined prayer is a 'Judicial Filing' that the enemy has no legal capacity to ignore."

4. "My child's identity is not a 'Work in Progress'; it is a 'Completed Verdict' rendered in the Courts of Zion before the world began.

5. "I have moved my seed from the 'Victim's List' to the 'Governor's Registry'; they are no longer subjects of the culture, but rulers over it."

6. "The 'Siphons' of my ancestors are broken, and the 'Momentum' of the fathers is now the 'Acceleration' of the sons."

7. "My home is a 'No-Fly Zone' for the kingdom of darkness and a 'High Pressure Gateway' for the angels of the Lord."

8. "I do not pray for 'Safety'; I pray for 'Expansion,' for my seed was born to possess the high places of the earth."

9. "The 'Unpolluted Well' of my child's creativity shall produce solutions that heal the waste places of many generations."

10."I am the Mother of Lions; my Roar is the end of the scavenger's reign and the beginning of the King's Dominion in my bloodline."

**About the Author - Dr. Philomena Gerald**
**Medical Doctor | Intercessor | Author | Kingdom Strategist**

Dr. Philomena Gerald Ishengoma is a Medical doctor, devoted wife and mother, and a commissioned intercessor with a global mandate for spiritual restoration and deliverance. She is the Founder and visionary leader of *Jesus Deliverance Clinic International Ministries*, a dynamic apostolic hub dedicated to healing, foundational reconstruction, and the enforcement of Kingdom authority.

With a rare integration of medical expertise and deep spiritual insight, Dr. Philomena operates at the intersection of clinical care and spiritual deliverance, addressing both physical conditions and foundational spiritual issues affecting individuals, families, and communities.

## Calling & Ministry Assignment

Dr. Philomena is widely recognized as the Convener of the *Midnight Battle Intercessory Prayer*, a strategic and prophetic movement that mobilizes believers to engage in targeted spiritual warfare. This platform emphasizes the execution of divine judgments, referred to as the **"Verdict of the Decree"**, against entrenched powers of darkness.

Her ministry assignment centers on:

- Restoring broken foundations
- Uprooting generational patterns and legal claims
- Equipping believers to function as Governors of Light
- Enforcing Kingdom laws through spiritual intelligence and prayer

**Her mission is clear:**
To transition the Body of Christ from subjects of circumstance into rulers of spiritual territory through deep foundational deliverance.

**The Library of Dr. Philomena Gerald**

**Strategies for Governance, Deliverance, and Kingdom Authority**

Dr. Philomena is a prolific author whose works serve as essential guides in deliverance ministry and spiritual jurisprudence. Her writings provide practical, structured frameworks for engaging spiritual warfare from a legal and governmental perspective.

## Featured Publications:

1. **Deep Foundational Deliverance**
   *Secret to Spiritual Warfare:* Identifying and uprooting hidden legal claims, ancestral covenants, and ancient cycles of defeat.

2. **Prayer Against Witchcraft: Overruled**
   *Dismantling Darkness:* Severe warfare prayers and judicial decrees against witchcraft, sorcery, evil altars, and demonic monitoring systems.

3. **Divine Eviction of Addiction**
   *Restoring the Temple:* Judicial prayers to break addiction, mental oppression, wasting spirits, trauma cycles, and premature death.

4. **Courts of Heaven (Vol. 1): From Defendant to Ruler**
   *The Governor's Brief:* Transitioning from spiritual victimhood into Kingdom authority through divine legal protocol.

5. **Courts of Heaven (Vol. 2): Silencing the Accuser**
   *Securing the Verdict:* Enforcing the judgments of Heaven, silencing satanic accusations, and maintaining spiritual victory.

6. **Children Daily Prayer Manual**
   *The Next Generation:* A 365-day Kingdom training

manual for raising spiritual leaders, royal priests, and Kingdom executives.

7. **Sex Before Marriage**
   *Foundational Corruption:* Breaking soul ties, covenant defilement, lust patterns, and restoring purity, identity, and covenant alignment.

8. **Family Foundational Deliverance**
   *Breaking Household Bondage:* Exposing inherited patterns, family altars, bloodline afflictions, and ancestral legal rights.

9. **The Praying Mother**
   *The Watchwoman's Mantle:* Intercessory strategies for mothers to preserve destinies, cover families in prayer, and establish godly bloodlines.

10. **Deliverance from Familiar Spirits**
    *Breaking Evil Familiarity:* Identifying and destroying monitoring spirits, inherited demonic patterns, spiritual impersonation, and satanic manipulation.

11. **Deliverance from Spirit Spouses**
    *Breaking Ungodly Covenants:* Deliverance prayers against spiritual marriages, dream pollution, covenant bondage, and marital delay.

www.ingramcontent.com/pod-product-compliance
Lightning Source LLC
LaVergne TN
LVHW010838120826
845149LV00017B/3296

* 9 7 9 8 9 9 5 3 8 6 1 1 7 *